SIX MONTHS IN KANSAS

SIX MONTHS IN KANSAS

By A Lady

(Mrs. Hannah Anderson Ropes)

The Black Heritage Library Collection

BOOKS FOR LIBRARIES PRESS
FREEPORT, NEW YORK
1972

First Published 1856
Reprinted 1972

Reprinted from a copy in the
Fisk University Library Negro Collection

INTERNATIONAL STANDARD BOOK NUMBER:
0-8369-8987-2

LIBRARY OF CONGRESS CATALOG CARD NUMBER:
76-38020

PRINTED IN THE UNITED STATES OF AMERICA
BY
NEW WORLD BOOK MANUFACTURING CO., INC.
HALLANDALE, FLORIDA 33009

SIX MONTHS

IN

KANSAS.

BOSTON:
PUBLISHED BY JOHN P. JEWETT AND CO.
CLEVELAND, OHIO:
JEWETT, PROCTOR AND WORTHINGTON.
NEW-YORK:
SHELDON, BLAKEMAN AND CO.
1856.

Entered according to Act of Congress, in the year 1856, by
JOHN P. JEWETT AND CO.,
In the Clerk's Office of the District Court of the District of Massachusetts.

LITHOTYPED BY THE AMERICAN STEREOTYPE COMPANY,
28 PHŒNIX BUILDING, BOSTON.

PRINTED BY D. S. FORD AND CO.

TO MY MOTHER,
WHOSE LIFE HAS BEEN MORE BEAUTIFUL THAN A POEM,
WISER THAN A PROVERB,
THESE LETTERS WERE WRITTEN.

TO ALL WHOM I LOVE
IN DEAR NEW ENGLAND;
TO THE MOTHERS
WHO AT DIFFERENT TIMES HAVE PUT ON A CHEERFUL COURAGE
TO SAY "FAREWELL" TO DEAR CHILDREN AND GRANDCHILDREN,
PUSHING FORTH TO THIS FAR-OFF LAND,
THEY ARE HERE TENDERLY AND AFFECTIONATELY
INSCRIBED.

LAWRENCE, Kansas Territory,
April, 1856.

H. A. R.

PREFACE.

The authoress went to Kansas in September, 1855, and returned to Massachusetts in April, 1856. During her absence she wrote the following letters to her mother, and, at the suggestion of her friends, they are here presented to the public, with but few alterations. She makes no pretensions to literary excellence, but asks the reader to remember the disadvantages under which these letters were written. The narrative is authentic.

April 1856.   H. A. R.

CONTENTS.

	PAGE
THE JOURNEY TO KANSAS,	9
FIRST EXPERIENCES IN KANSAS,	45
THE MISSOURI INVASION,	95
MURDER OF BARBOUR — THE TRUCE,	129
WINTER EXPERIENCES AND OBSERVATIONS,	153
KANSAS SUFFERERS — TROUBLE THREATENED,	182
MISCELLANEOUS LETTERS,	207

SIX MONTHS IN KANSAS.

JOURNEY TO KANSAS.

SEPTEMBER 11, 1855.

DEAR MOTHER, — We are outside of Boston, feeling something like unweaned chickens, whose heads, if not wrung off, are at the best, worse for a blow. I notice the last guide-board says "Ashland." Now surely the smell is no longer the villainous odor of the Depot neighborhood; or the noise, the rattling over Boston pavements. We are among the green fields, making a great steam and noise on our own account, and borne along — as it is sometimes good to be, by the submissiveness of our own will — by the fretting power of an engine. Our speed is not extreme however, and there is a murmur through the cars, that we are behind the time. Men grumble and consult their watches often; they wish to take a night train. We who stop at Albany do not care so much. The heat is very oppressive and the dust covers us. Thanks to sister Eliza for the napkins in our basket. In the car is a water-tank; we wet the napkins and wipe our faces, hands, and necks. How it cools and refreshes us! The napkins give proof what color we are, by their own dingy aspect. We rinse them, and dry them on the window-sill.

The sun has been staring us in the face for a long·time, as though he would look us out of countenance for running away from home. What a flood of glory about him! I feel a little rebuked at his unwinking stare. I muster up from my memory all the reasons wherewith I nerved myself to leave dear New England; but they do not stand out so clearly as when first enrolled in my cause. Like me, they seem wilted by the heat and marred by the noise.

But now the sun has gone down, and we are in Springfield — that is to say, in Springfield Depot. I hope no one ever gave out word that he had seen a city or a town after whisking through the back side of it in the cars. We stop here for another train to pass, and to take in fuel. The lights are set burning, people gather back again into their seats and make themselves comfortable after their own fashion. Men have suddenly grown shorter. There is nothing of them in fact. Coat collars have gone up in a most ambitious manner; hats have settled down humbly; there is nothing of them but the crowns. Here and there, also, the smallest apology for a knee braced against the seat, or palpable evidence of boots hanging midway over the seat's end, make it rather a hazardous excursion through the alley-way.

Our party numbers twenty-five, ten of them children, and five women, who are going to homes prepared for them and now occupied by their husbands and fathers. The babies are now quiet with the exception of one, a stout, healthful child of two years, such as Barnum would rejoice in as an article of speculation. The mother is a gentle, attractive woman, occupying a seat next to ours. How she is to get through this journey with the care of a child so heavy, is yet to be seen. Every time the cars stop, little Ella sets up a cry of indignation and injured innocence. It is electrical: there is a spasmodic motion between the hat-crowns and boots, accompanied with a smothered grumbling sound, lost in the onward progress of the cars. Little Ella is satisfied; flings up her arms, throws out her plump feet in a most jaunty manner, and passes into the land of dreams, unmindful of the weary, aching pain in her mother's arms. Was there ever anything so ludicrous as a car of sleeping passengers by lamplight, tossed hither and yon by the incessant motion? Beautiful little Ella, you are the brightest of us all under the circumstances. The nodding spirit is upon me; and, so my dear mother, good night.

Sept. 12*th.* — The hope of a good night's rest at Albany, kept us up till eleven o'clock. We were stiff and tired, and the children cross, as they had a right to be, waked up at that time of night. We went from the cars to the boat; from the boat into the dark night, through a silent street, entering, at last, doors which seemed to open in walls, and to lead nowhere, until steps were mounted, which seemed endless and hard to be got over. But they were at length finished, and we found ourselves in a dimly-lighted parlor, long, narrow, and low, with a parlor carpet of otter color and muddy green, woven into frightful contortions of diamonds and squares:—a midnight-looking apartment, where company was not expected nor prepared for.

Chairs were brought, enough for all; the gas was turned up more brilliantly; a pitcher of water and one tumbler were procured; the hands of the timepiece pointed to twelve. O, how tired we were! would the clerk never show us our beds? He came in very pleasantly, and remarked, with as much composure as though he was speaking of the weather: "Every bed in the house is full,—you must make yourselves comfortable till breakfast time!"

Twenty-five of us in one room, after riding from Boston! My first twinge of homesickness was at Springfield when the sun went down. I now felt another spasm. The children were cross, the mothers in despair, the little woman with the big baby looked as though she would faint.

My first thought was of personal injustice;

the second was more practical. I took up the bundle of shawls, which had been such a trouble to us when we changed cars, feeling amply paid, in the wealth of help they now gave to make others comfortable. One was speedily folded into a mattress, and as the chairs were stuffed haircloth, by thrusting my hand under one, it readily slipped out from the frame. It was speedily transferred to a corner of the room, the shawl covered over it, and the pale little woman laid away upon it for the remaining night-time, while the big baby, Ella, was spread in my lap, to be hushed off to sleep by the scraps of baby lullabies still lingering in my memory, as sung by you when I was young. What a splendid great child! How did that mother live through so long a ride and this child in her arms?

The room was long, fortunately. The male portion of the party soon settled off into one end of it, with chair-bottoms for pillows; and the women gradually spread themselves among the children, prophesying that they could not sleep, but yet yielding at last to "tired nature's sweet restorer;" and the children, too, did not, I presume, know the difference between his night and any other of their lives, tent minutes after they lay about the floor. They never sentimentalize.

When the time pointed to two o'clock, baby Ella was laid beside her mother; the rocking-chair back laid upon the floor; my cloak spread in it, and with little Alice, kitten-like rolled up by my side, I took my first lesson in Kansas camping. It was not half as bad as I expected. A night, even on the floor, will come to an end; ours did not commence till midnight, and morning light came in at the usual time. Our women looked quite tired out, and not a little ill-used; but a good breakfast brightened us all up, and at half-past seven we took to the cars again.

Consider us going back through those doors in curious places, the mystery attendant upon them all dispersed by daylight; ten small children, one more than the martyr Rogers had. Surely we were martyrs, what with the carpet-bags, the shawls, basket of provision, a child of our own, or of some other mother, tugging at our skirts, with incessant injunctions "not to let go," "not to walk so slow," the clamorous outcries of every other body, or party, in which of course we had no especial interest, and to whom we were quite unwilling to waive any rights or privileges. The sudden determination to mount the car-steps, (were there ever any so high from the ground before?) two children and one mother abreast, carpet-bag and basket included, pocket, too, filled with apples, et cetera — of course was a failure, and of course you took up the time of the next body behind; and yet, you find yourself *thrown*, as it were, up those awful steps, into the cars, by the terror of the oath in the rear, at your delay. Blessed be the proprieties of cars on such occasions; the refuge of the seats; the breeze stirred by their outward-bound motion. I take a long breath at the safety of us all. I turn round to congratulate the little woman upon our triumph over difficulties, and she is not there. My heart is in my mouth. If she is not here, she cannot be in safety; who can take thought for her but me, with so much of their own to look after? I look over all my matters, as if to make sure that I have not appropriated her with the baby, as a portion of my luggage. There sits Alice in the safe corner, but she could hardly hover even a little woman. As for Ella, she is not of the sort to be hovered, now or at any future time. I conjure up the picture of her, left behind in that bedlam of a Depot. What is to be done? ah, there comes the knight-errant of our party. I will report. He makes a rapid tramp through the whole train, and returns; she is safe! My heart settles down in its place, making the resolve, to look better after her in future.

Now then for a peep at the country — Central New York, with its fine farms, its hills, reminding one so much of the best cultivated portions of Maine; its canals, bearing along little arks, such as the old primer gave to us in a wood-cut of quaint device, as the especial model of Noah's; its immense fields of broomcorn, hanging its richly-tasselled heads in most wondrous profusion! Ah, it was all very beautiful, and to me new; but the dearest memento I treasure in my memory of our ride through central New York, is the mullenstalk, by the wayside. A rough and hairy leaf it has, a tall and coarse blossom and seed-vessel; but down in the old pasture-lane we used to gather them at your command, my mother, to be hung in the garret, as a panacea when winter brought us sore throats. I take my last peep at the mullen-stalk in New York. I'm brave enough to say, it has stirred more emotion, more lasting thought within me, than anything I shall trace again to day.

Evening picks us up at ——; we are to travel all night. It rains, and the air is very close. We get tea, and beg the privilege of getting into the cars, though they do not start for two hours. This time, we are fortunate enough to get seats together. I have tucked away the luggage for the night. Two young men of our party sit in front of us, and relieve me of the valise and carpet-bag. What a nice bed we have made. Alice is asleep. Little Ella, too, has dispensed with the motion of the cars for once, and lies opposite, at full length. The company have all settled off into a quiet sleep. I hear a smothered sound, a gasp like Susie's when she fell down in the night by my bedside in a fainting fit. So much asleep am I, that it is difficult to convince myself I am not going over another edition of that scene in a dream.

O dear! the little woman has fainted! She is in my arms. What a wake up there is! Even boots find their level on the floor; windows that no one had strength to open, are thrown up without discussion; private little brandy-bottles suddenly appear from the most innocent-looking carpet-bags, and from the most staid-looking women. What a world of kind feeling a faint, even, will bring to the surface of the most indifferent group, when it is needed. I decide to keep to this woman till she has a little sleep. Every body goes off again; the danger is over; she sleeps quietly in my arms; while, with my feet, I keep romping Miss Ella, from rolling on to the floor.

Thursday morning, long before you are up, the cars make a ten-minutes stop in Her Majesty's dominions; and you can fancy me stepping out to an eating house, with my miniature tea-pot in hand, to get it filled with hot tea. I go at a venture, for they sell it only to breakfast-eaters; but it was a kindly-looking woman whom I addressed, and she gave orders to the servant to "fill it to the full, with as much milk and sugar as the lady liked." Heaven bless her! I shall probably never see her again; and should I, I could not recognize her, but by her voice. She gave me more than a "cup of cold water"— a warm and inspiring cup of tea, after a sleepless night ending in a lonesome, cloudy morning; and she shall have her "reward."

Our ride in Canada was through a beautiful tall wood, and upon high table-land, level as possible. As we neared the lake, the country was level to painfulness. Water and shore a continuous plain, and water the color of dirty soapsuds. If all the lake-shore scenery is like this, I have seen all I care to see.

Now we whirl along opposite Detroit. It is a pleasant break upon the monotony, as we near the ferry-boat. A few moments bring us to the (to me, *awful*) depot proximity. All sorts of unearthly sounds are about us; and people of every nation seem to be hurrying west.

It seems as though one train of cars could never swallow up all these people. Six of our party are seated. The baggage is not all on board. Our conductor is resolute, and will not leave it, and calls for us to get out. I have only time to put Alice out, my foot is on the step, there is a bedlam noise, when the cars start off as though they were mad, with me standing in a bewildered maze, with my hand on the door, my eyes gazing deep into that now superlatively awful depot, where little Alice, basket in hand, mother's cloak safe on her arm, stands demurely, with her own expression of sweet content quite unruffled. One of the young knight-errants of the party leads me back to my seat, and says, "They will be on in the next train." My seat looks too lonely for any long ride. I look round for some one acquainted with the road. There is a face close by; it is very intent upon a newspaper, but it looks up kindly to the question, "When will the next train leave Detroit for Joiliet?" and he was sorry to tell me, I should not see little Alice till the next day! Now the blood leaps quickly, and thought is all astir. Wait till to morrow? No! Getchel is the prince of lads. We get out at the first station, we wait an hour, we take the next train back, and find all taking a comfortable dinner at a hotel. She said all the while, " Mother will come back," and at the sound of the car-whistle, came down to meet me.

At five o'clock we took seats for Illinois; rode all night at a furious rate; got out at Lake Station before daylight, and were huddled into a dirty room, to wait till seven. I have seen nothing clean to eat, drink, or sit or stand upon, for some time. If there was only a rock somewhere, that would, in the very nature of it, refuse to become impregnated with this universal nastiness; or, one of those glorious old walls, built by our grandfathers, running in curious crooks and turns up and down their domains, to which the dearest little mossy forests cling, and upon which many a weary wayfarer makes a seat, in the dust of travel, or to get ease from pain, when daylight deepens into darkness!

Fields of corn there are, rich in promise, and in extent immense. Now, too, the grand beauty of prairie scenery dawns upon us. It is quite impossible to give you any idea of its wonderful expanse, — the innumerable herds of cattle, sheep, and horses, whose distance from us can only be measured by their diminished size; and the flowers— O, how beautiful and numberless!— such as you grow in gardens, are here sown broadcast, by luxurious nature's hand, in a most happy combination of colors, yellow, white, and purple. This is payment indeed, for the previous fatigue. I am only homesick, to-day, when we come to some of the most miserable apologies for towns ever set forth in station-books.

On the open prairie, one has nature, in the open space of fields unfenced, in the wide over-hanging sky, all to one's self. There is no need for talk; words jar upon the ear when the eye leads the emotions of beauty captive. The farm-houses, and hay-ricks, speck the distance, as ships the sea. They do not interrupt the harmony; they are a part of the beautiful picture. But I could feel no more at home on a prairie, than on the sea; there is nothing individual about either.

When we arrived at Alton, darkness had settled down about us for the night; so that we saw nothing by which to remember the flourishing town, always associated in my mind with the murder of Lovejoy, twenty years since.

From the cars, we were transferred to a steamer, plying between Alton and St. Louis, twenty miles distant; thence to a carriage waiting on a muddy levee for us, under a driving rain; thence to a hotel. We were all very much in the condition of David Copperfield, when Mr. Dick suggested a "bath." And after securing a chamber, the next request was for the use of a bathing-room, which the house unfortunately did not possess. Water, however, was brought in abundance. Already the anticipated treat was prepared for, when, imagine the astonishment with which we witnessed the dropping into the basin a liquid precisely the color of dirty soap-suds! What was to be done? I sat down to decide which was the dirtiest, we three-days travellers in the heat and dust, or this forlorn dip from the Mississippi. As if to help me to a right decision, I went to the bowl and took a new survey. The liquid had certainly settled; the mud was not more than a finger deep at the bottom, and the basin was large. Now, then, I poured it off as carefully as you would cream from a pan of milk, until the stir of the mud bade me stop. You should have seen me, mother of mine, squatted on the floor at midnight, comparing those two bowls. I could have cried at the remembrance of all the pebbly-bottomed, clear streams I had left in dear New England. Now, one bowl looked like the mud-cakes we children used to stir with a stick, in broken china, and spread in fancy forms of cakes, pies, and turn-overs, on the cellar window-frame facing the sunny bank of the old house. What had been poured off was a poor edition of the rinsing water which old Rachel used to be so choice of in the tubs standing under the well-sweep.

But the escape from the *first* condition seemed so great, by comparison, that actual refreshment and rest followed an ablution in the second. To be sure I *did* dream of wading in dirty water, and working hard to dig a well in a sand-bar; but the morning found me laughing at my unsuccessful labors, and also busy with the preparation to go on board the steamer " Golden State, Capt. John Gonsullis," bound up the Missouri to Kansas

City, and other landings. The rain poured in torrents. St. Louis looked like a dirty slattern, as we drove to the boat; and the temperature was that of a close August day at home.

Everything seemed new. " Old things," had indeed passed away. Half the faces we saw were black. The horses seemed to have run quite entirely to ears and tails; and such queer looking carriages! The boat was another kind of thing, too, from ours at home. It looked all out of the water, and on that account awkward. The saloon is one hundred and thirty feet long, with nice little state-rooms on each side, opening not only into the saloon, but also on to the deck, with a blind to that door through which you can get whatever of air there may be astir, with the strictest privacy to your apartment at the same time.

The weather is intolerably hot. I never felt anything like it. We have three dozen children on board. This saloon is the sitting-room and eating-room combined. The children have no resort, not even at meal-time; and as the passengers are mostly families of emigrants, who are supposed not to be very rich, the children, have not, of course, any nurses but their tired-looking mothers. There are passengers, too, from Kentucky, Indiana, Illinois and Alabama; well-bred, and ill-bred, gentle and simple. There is a large family of newly bought slaves — children, with their parents. I do not know where they pass their time days. My first view of them, or knowledge of their existence, was on going into the saloon quite late. The floor was quite covered with dark faces, sound asleep, of every age and size, down to plump and happy sleeping infancy. We have colored waiters, twenty or more, as well drilled as soldiers. The table is spread with great variety and abundance at every meal; and the motion of a boat over "six feet scant" of water, is not sufficient to destroy the appetite.

Sept. 14*th.* — The Sabbath has been very quiet on board. Prayer books are in the hands of many of the passengers and boatmen. I have watched with some curiosity the different elements that-settle off in eddies. I hear some snapping of small-arms between the slavery and anti-slavery commons. There is not a good spirit shown on either side. The subject is very great, but the combatants are puny; they cannot look over it fairly, because they are not tall enough; or at each other justly, because they are prejudiced. A David, with a sling and trifling stone, could aim with effect where these fail with loud and angry words.

O dear, I wish they would not *talk*. I believe I hate petty argument. It leaves each stronger in his own view. But perhaps it is because I am a woman, and, woman-like, jump to a conclusion without the drudgery of measuring the intermediate steps.

Now, the aspect of things at the upper end of the saloon changes for the better. There is the voice of a woman surely; others are calmed by it. The voice is very sweet, and the face a goodly one; the dialect purely New England. I have noticed this woman often: her face is remarkably fine; her person large, and well proportioned; she has two fine boys with her, to make Kansas men of; and she goes to meet her husband. Happy woman! Her manner is simple; her words without extravagance. Like oil, they smooth the rumpled feathers of antagonism. She explains how, without being paupers, we emigrate in companies, for better security against homesickness, and for the continuance of New England institutions. Mother, she is just such a woman as you would like. Such as, sitting in the shade of her home, even though it be but a rude cabin or a tent, will, through her children, tell upon the character of the next generation with a force greater than that of half a dozen "women of strong minds."

There are sitting near me, two gentlemen and three ladies from Kentucky, and slave-owners. I like them, to look at. The young ladies have been drawn to the upper end of the saloon. There is an honest interest in their faces, aside from the good breeding, which makes them attentive listeners. The young man of the party, a fine specimen of a man, has also drawn his chair within hearing distance. The discussion has changed its character. Supper has come in season to dissolve the gathering, before bitterness again springs up.

The old gentleman from the South introduces himself to me after tea. He wishes to ask me questions about the north. He feels her superiority, he says; but he wishes we better understood the difficulty of their position, who are born to the inheritance of slaves. He is one who voted for gradual emancipation; but the bill was lost. These are people of the old school of good breeding; and my talk with them is one of the pleasantest rays on the sand-bars of the Missouri.

A very faint idea of this fickle, deceitful *Miss* of the west can you form, without floating within her shores for a few days. There is no such thing as hurry, upon her waters. Put on steam, and set forth to drive a "fast team," and the circumstance which will make you white in the face, and faint at heart, will be the fangs of a "snag" driven into the keel; or the drifts of an unseen sand-bar on either side.

At table, I sit at the right hand of the Captain. The bell is rung the moment he appears at the farther end of the saloon, and every waiter watches the slightest motion of his hand, or eye. In his personal appearance, there is both dignity and authority; and at table, the wants of every person are noticed by him, at a glance. He has passed the most of his life upon this river; and makes one at the wheel of his boat, passing most of his time there. He invites us up to pass an hour with him, after the sun is down. The view is really beautiful at times. The shores are thickly wooded, with the general appearance of an uninhabited country. Occasionally, there are grand columns of sand-stone, giving a good idea of ivy covered towers in the old world. The channel of the river is never in the same place twice; and as the water is muddy, it is a continued wonder how a way is ciphered out by the Captain, at the wheel.

It is just a week since we left home, and we are three hundred and fifty miles up this river. It seems endless, and the immensity just begins to dawn upon me, as well as the distance from home. No place have I seen yet where I could make a home. Everything seems a world too wide for the home emotion to root in. Crack goes the boat, with a prolonged grate beneath her, as though she was scraped in pieces! Mother, we are on a sand-bar, and perhaps may pass a week here.

Five hours! The moon is up brightly. The boat's crew, after most exhausting efforts, have pushed her off into four feet of water. She moves heavily, and as though contending with a power by which she has once been vanquished. Everybody is standing near the railing looking over anxiously. The mate is the most villianous rascal I ever saw. How he does treat those tired sailors. Every second word is an oath, uttered in the voice of a fiend, and accompanied often with the weight of his hand or foot.

Now, two men are standing one on either side of the lower deck, sounding. Their voices go up cheerfully, or sadly, as the lead sinks more or less. Their report is taken up by another man, leaning over the third deck, and thus reaches the captain, at the wheel, up still another story, mid-ships. When the report sends forth the sound, "four feet large," then everybody says, we shall get on, our notions of water being at ebb tide just now.

The river here is very broad, with prominent sand-bars here and there, of an acre or more in extent. Nearer the opposite shore is another steamer, fast in the mud. Her passengers, are troops for fort Riley. She is a mile from us, but a common curse makes us friends. We steer towards her, still sounding as before. We *pass* her. Her crew forget their own dilemma in our release, and cheer us.

We are now over the worst bars of the river. At twelve in the night we reach Lexington, and part company with our Southern friends, not without regret. To-morrow we have the promise of being in Kansas city.—To-morrow has come. We gather up the scattered fragments of our wardrobe in our berths. The little woman leans over the rail at my open door; she looks pale; we quarrel about the expediency of her taking rest, in anticipation of the fatigue of to-morrow. I go my way, she takes hers. In less than half an hour, I am sent for, verily she has fainted entirely! I send to the bar for iced wine. There is not a breath of air cooler than that which blows from a furnace. There is no motion about her heart; but she looks earnestly at me, while I feed her with the wine. A gentleman passenger from Connecticut, with rare chivalry, takes entire care of the big baby. Why does she have these turns? Is it fatigue, or excitement at leaving dear New England? Toward sun-down she seems quite recovered. We hail Kansas City in the distance, looking really more pleasant than one could anticipate; and glad we all are to anticipate a release from the river, or at any rate a change. Kansas City stands upon a clay bluff, very steep, with one dirty street along near the landing, the hill towering roughly above it.

We passed the night comfortably; and as early as teams could be procured, started towards Kansas Territory. Our carriage was a cart, covered with sail-cloth, not quite high enough to allow us to sit with our heads up. There were nine of us to two mules, beside the driver. We rode up round the hill at the peril of our necks, expressed by the female portion of the party in sudden starts and broken screams. The sun came out intensely hot; then we began to make love to the ugly sail-cloth and draw it closely down about us.

We came into the Indian country after riding about seven miles from Kansas City. The road, with the exception of occasional ravines, with slight runs of water through their bottoms, is remarkably fine—winding in most picturesque curves through open, unfenced prairie and grand old oak groves, as free from underbrush as a gentleman's well-kept grounds, with trees such as make the Saxon blood quicken at their height and antiquity.

There is one point here which I can never forget, midway between Kansas City and the extreme border of the Shawnee Reserve. After walking down a steep ravine, crossing the creek on stones, climbing the opposite bank, tired, and out of breath, we packed away again in the cart, and the faithful mules started off briskly, up, up, a long way. We then came into a broad mowing field of a thousand acres —smooth as a lawn, but by no means a dead level; not a fence to be seen, nor a habitation. The sun lay at our right, nearly down; but he did not cheat us, as he often does at home, by the device of a hill close at hand, behind which he seems to look over to say, with the familiarity of a near neighbor, " Good night." No indeed, there was nothing so cozy about this scene. Grand, beyond all conception it was, but stern and distant, like the life of the understanding without affection. In the midst of the awe with which it inspired us there opened before us another view of the same picture — at some distance appeared a gentle rise, continuous for a mile or more, and stretching far to the right and left, a perfect lawn, studded everywhere with groups and belts of those tall oaks, graceful in arrangement, perfect in growth. We jumped up — we shouted, with the newly awakened delight of tired and homesick children. But there was no response from human voice. Our ardor exhausted itself; the road wound gently down, leaving this part of the wilderness on our left, and the grand spread mowing field, with the golden sun light, on our right. Our way now ran along the dull prose of a country road, settling us back into the full consciousness of the cart — its sailcloth covering knocking against our bonnets at every jolt; its plank seats without backs; its cramped, uncomfortable crowdedness of people, of children, of baskets, of carpet-bags, of cloaks and shawls; its sickening odor of crumbled gingerbread, of bread and butter, of cheese and dried beef. And now, the deepening twilight makes every soul turn with struggling yearning to the thought of home.

Ah me, Mother of mine! "What went we out into the wilderness for to see? A reed shaken with the wind?" Every heart in these emigrant wagons has its history, and is treading its wine press alone. How, to the outward observer, we seem lifted, whether we will or not, by the hard and rough winds of circumstances, and borne along the high road of human life; drifting, it may be, into some quiet, sheltered, cosey corner; or, out where we should least expect to find ourselves — amidst immeasurable difficulties of position.

Silence has fallen upon our party. It looks like a company of nuns, in whom all emotion was smothered long ago, till it had died. But not so really. Old Memory has taken us by the shoulders and turned us round. We are all scattered to our own homes that were. And where is mine, my dear Mother, if not with you? So I am in your room, to greet you as you come in after tea. You hold the little hand-lamp in one hand, and you are very careful to secure the latch of the door with the other; how you place the unlighted lamp on the right hand corner of the mantleshelf, and with a care-taking glance over the room, to see

that all is in order, sink into the easy chair
under it. I am sitting opposite you, looking
into your earnest eyes; you look pale and
slightly sad; you gaze into the cheerful wood
fire; your elbow rests upon your knee, and
you make an easy chair of the hand and wrist,
into which, by the right of former possession,
your chin settles down comfortably. Now you
slily adjust the spinal weakness of the immense
brass andiron nearest you, (by the way, I
always felt that you considered yourself responsible for the good appearance of that unfortunate member of the family,) and with the
hearth-brush you make an attempt at fighting
up some stray ashes or coals; as though they
had not learned long ago better than to touch
so nice a hearth-stone. Those bright old and-
irons, how they belong to home! and the
shovel and tongs that never knock their heads
into the jams, nor irreverently roll over with
a clattering sound; the two quaint candlesticks
of the same metal, standing so as to measure
the length of the snuffer tray, which always
occupies the centre of the mantel. Now you
light a taper, and the candle which is longest
is set burning. The knitting suddenly appears,

and you are busy. The shadows flicker over the room, for your one wax is not brilliant. I lift the veil from the living picture of our dear old father; pass my hand also to the fancy piece from the hand of a dear sister, who thus prepared a tablet for her own name; I smooth my hand along the household stuff of a past century, which, in the old ballad words, "the more it is used the brighter it shines;" I take a gaze again at the venerable face, the erect form, which has borne the care of four score years without growing old and childish. The whole atmosphere of your presence has rested me, and now I say, "Good night, mother," for it seems as though you were at my elbow. "Good bye, dear New England. Was there no hearth vacant and sad by my absence? Was there no cabin within your precincts into which I could enter by a *fee simple?*"

"There," shouts the driver, "don't you see there!" We jump up with a shiver, and, as in duty bound, look. We see, far in the distance, what appears like a respectable-sized barn, forming a step between the frightfully wide country and the clear glowing horizon. We ask, "What is it?"

"Well now," says he of the whip, "It 'pears like you don't know nothing of these parts. Why, that's Paschal Fish's, where we puts up."

"How far is it from this?"

"O, a mile and a bit or so."

We never knew how long the "mile" measured; but the "bit" was a dangerous extension of time, prostration of our tired nerves, and a stripping to shreds of our pretty-well-worn patience.

The driver tried to beguile the way by telling us about Paschal Fish, an Indian of the Shawnee tribe, and of power among them. A very honest man, don't drink a drop of whiskey, has a corn-field of a hundred acres, and thirty acres of oats; keeps a little store, and employs New England men to make the sales; turns his house into a sort of a tavern, and employs a Yankee to cook for his company.

Paschal sits with his hat on, in a ruminating mood, the most of the time—welcomes New England people—says, "We saw the cloud in the east, one, two, three summers ago, and now it is beginning to come upon us." Here ends the driver's prattle. We are at the door of this *new hotel.*

We dismount, and enter at the only door into the first story of a large building, simply boarded and loosely floored. It is dimly lighted with poor tallow candles in Japan candlesticks, which bear evidence of having been the support of candles before. There is a long table in the floor, and men, in whose faces there is absolutely no mouth to be seen, and only a gleam for eyes, — an entire party of heads, covered with dirty, uncombed, unwashed hair. There were no more chairs. Our baggage was brought in, and we made seats of it. The men ate as though the intricacies from their plates to their mouths had become a perfect slight of hand with them. As they passed out of the room, the dishes were wiped out for us!

Soon we passed up a staircase, in one end of the room, creaking and bending beneath our weight, as though we were not safe. The floor above was of the same stamp as that below, — one thin board of cotton-wood, which is somewhat like willow. In the loft there was a cotton-cloth partition. I was fortunate enough to secure a place for Alice in a good bed, with the wife of a physician, and drew close before the tented door a narrow, cross-bedstead, having no bed upon it, and only a blanket for clothing. I made a pillow of my travelling-bag, and laid myself away for the night. It was the best bed I had seen, for there were no occupants but myself.

Now, men, in single file, marched up and spread themselves over most of the outer floor. Sleep fell down upon these waifs of humanity. The house was quiet; and the new day greeted us all with the blessing of a clear sky before our sleep was over.

Before we were well awake, the male department was vacated. Now came the always-recurring desire for water, and the hopelessly small portion to be obtained. One tin basin was most respectfully waited for, and the square of looking-glass patiently held by each one in turn, till our eyes were washed and our hair set a little smooth. As for teeth, we could not raise anything to rinse them with, till I thought of my little mug in the basket. With a sort of smoothed-down travelling aspect, we went down over the stairs. There sat Paschal Fish, hat over his eyes, legs crossed, looking as though he had not moved all night.

The room looked pleasanter. Most of the travellers had gone. A bright and cheerful face, grown quite familiar from having been one among our party, was assuming some of the cares which belonged to the cook, who, it appeared, was her husband. She gave us clean and shining cups, saucers, and plates. She brought us hot biscuit from the oven — just the smell of which made us hungry — and coffee, such as I never found at any hotel before. Her husband served three years at Myers', and the coffee was a credit to his teachers.

After such a breakfast, we were quite in good humor, and mounted into the old cart, almost as good as new. Nine miles more we were to ride before we pitched our tents.

The country did not seem as truly beautiful coming towards Lawrence city. The Wabarusa was nearly dry, and we rode down into its bed and up the opposite bank, which was frightfully steep. Then we came to a little settlement, called Franklin, entirely bare of trees and shrubs. This open, unbroken waste of nothing but grass, with a sprinkling of little cabins, is inharmonious to my mind. We notice plenty of cows feeding along the way, among this wealth of grass, and, beside most of the cabins, ricks of hay, stacked for the winter's feed. Meanwhile, our eyes look earnestly forward for the first indication of the town of Lawrence. At our left, far off, the hills rise grandly, terrace-like, one back of the other, — and so green and smooth! Our driver calls the most prominent one, "Blue Mound," where the prophets of these tribes see fine college buildings looming in the years of Kansas' glory and prosperity.

Soon this little wisp of a man tells us to "Come down from the mountains," and look at the city at our feet. One could hardly conceive of a picture so really *beautiful*, of a town one year old. As we enter, the river — which we do not see — forms the background, with its thickly-wooded bank. A few nice-looking houses appear, and cabins quite numberless. We ride to the door of the Cincinnati House. And now, my dear mother, my journey is over. I tie my knot, and, with a nervous, trembling hand, say, good-bye. Keep the corner for me warm, because I shall prove, like the dove of old, a returner to the old ark.

H. A. R.

FIRST EXPERIENCES.

SEPTEMBER 20TH, 1855.

MY DEAR MOTHER: — I closed my last letter, and bade you good-bye, quite in a hurry. But as soon as I had entered the "Cincinnati House," I cast around to discover, if possible, some nice, quiet little corner, where I could tuck myself away, and, with a pencil, take notes for you. The "young lad" who drew us out here had gone out to a claim early in the morning, and would not return till late.

The house into which we entered appeared outside, and perhaps within, very much like the way-station depots at home, — made of boards, jointed and painted dark brown, containing two square rooms, with an attache at the back end, of a ten-footer, looking like a wen on the side of a man's neck, but really a cooking-room. The two rooms are plastered, one making a nice parlor and the other a dining-room. There are two chambers over them; and, above all, a perfectly flat roof.

On the same lot, directly in the rear, is a barn-looking building, with four small rooms below, each having a door opening outside; a flight of stairs running up at the end, into four little attics. Each of these rooms has *slatted* walls, floors, and bedsteads, and is designed to receive (I will not say accommodate) three persons. I am thus particular in my description because I have had a great deal to do with these rooms, and I wish all your sympathy with everything I experience. The parlor is furnished with one table, small, oval-shaped, hewn out from the beautiful black walnut of the country; one rocking-chair, and three lounges, made of round sticks of unpealed wood, over which is stretched cotton cloth, of rather uncertain firmness of fabric, giving one the idea of breaking through. They are stuffed with prairie grass, and nicely covered with patch.

This house is kept by two clever women from Lowell; one of whom kept a boarding-house there, and the other, as an operative, commended herself to some literary celebrity as Editress of the " Lowell Offering." The last mentioned person lay upon one of these lounges, sick with Typhoid fever. The other bore the marks of recent sickness, from which she considered herself recovering.

The "party" starting with us from Boston had spread away in every direction, except the fine woman with the two boys. Her destination was Topeka, and she had to wait till her husband sent for her. The sun had come out hot—hot as it could be. There was no water that we could relish, even to wash us in; and we were stinted, necessarily, to the smallest possible quantity. I never saw a woman so homesick as this mother of the boys. Her strength was entirely exhausted and she could not rest at all, but broke forth in the most clamorous complaints.

In the kitchen there was a pretty girl from New England, called Phebe, and a stout, good humored 'Susie,' from Illinois. One acted as waiter; the latter as cook—her business, I think she understood about as well as a freshly caught Laplander would have done. Then, there was Henry, and John, and David, who, each and all, served when there was a "rush" of company, or the water cask was dry.

I believe that the first thing which impressed

me, as people passed in and out, was the sickly look of everybody. All elasticity seemed to have been drawn away from them. Not being able to make myself or Alice particularly comfortable, I turned to Typhoid fever; straightened out the hair a little, washed the face and hands, worked the folds from its clothing, and Typhoid smiled gratefully upon me. I never could remember how, after dinner, I fell into a deep sleep, upon one of those lounges. At any rate, as the sun was going down, a hand pressed my head, and a voice said, "Wake up, sick one." The eyes opened as if by magic. Kneeling on the floor beside me was Ned, dressed in a clean pink and white shirt, thrown open loosely at the neck, sleeves rolled up above the elbow, boots drawn up over his pantaloons; face, neck, and arms brown, or rather, yellow as his hair. Typhoid turned her face to the wall, and wiped her eyes with the corner of her shawl. Phebe was in the door under her sun-bonnet, with flushed cheek. She looked astonished to find the "ice man" of sufficient consequence to bring us all the way from dear New England. How beautiful her face is!

Now we started out to see the cabin, which he said was but forty rods distant. The location is particularly pretty, on a rising mound, and looking down the river quite a distance. The cabin is fifteen feet square, and eleven feet high, giving room for quite a loft. The windows were cotton cloth; and the door was made of a frame, with a cross-piece, covered with the same material, having quite an extensive wooden latch fastened to the cross-piece with a wooden pin, and lifted from the outside by a twisted string. The cabin is made by driving joists into the ground four feet apart, and nailing "oak shakes" outside, after the manner of clapboards at home. These shakes are split out with an axe, after the blocks are sawed the proper length. This oak is a hard and crooked wood; and the shakes, as a matter of necessity, refrain from a very close embrace, leaving little scollops and curious bends, through which, in the night time, the stars can take a peep at us and we at them as well. There were six boards stretched across the middle of the room; and on one side a plank was fastened for a work bench. Overhead, as many more crooked, miserable-looking boards were drawn along, on which, with a buffalo skin and blanket a-piece, Ned and a young friend laid themselves away at night to sleep. Half a dozen of Sharpe's rifles, with plenty of ammunition, and a drum to sound an alarm, made up the chamber furniture. A rude ladder stood against the wall, to afford access to the upper story.

This was all the work of Ned's hands; and at an outlay of sixty dollars, beside his labor! Shakes are two dollars a hundred; good boards thirty-five dollars a thousand. The want of comfortable shelter is the great drawback to new comers, and causes fearful sickness.

I went back to the hotel, feeling as though I could not sleep in a room where half of it was the open ground. My terror of snakes, mice, and vermin generally, sprang into the most intense life; and would not be put down or reasoned with. The house was very full, and the barn too. Susie and Phebe slept upon the floor, in the room with four of us. Wearily we laid ourselves away, failing to find a chair, trunk, or even a nail, to spread our clothes upon. But the bed felt soft to us, and we had faith still left in the power to sleep, even under difficulties.

It is written, "Ye know not what shall be on the morrow." Verily, no fertile imaginings of your daughter could have conjured up the torture to be applied to her on this initiatory night in the new territory. Mother, in the first place, did you ever see a FLEA? Don't consider the question impertinent; or as throwing reproach upon your most respectable housekeeping. I ask for information; because I *have*. And on this night, when I imagined no enemy was near, they took sole possession of us all! I think I always had some respect for mosquitoes; they give warning always of their approach, and their note is unmistakably *bloody;* and a cheap bar over the bed secures you from everything but the cry for "blood." Quite another sort of villain is this black, shambling, hydra-legged "varmint;" using his legs only to leap with; never walking off, as though he had rights, but sneaking up from the floor just as one hopes to take possession of a bed, paid for, whisking in between the sheets in columns. Yet, put your finger on one of them if you can! Settle down and

close your eyes, for you are *so* tired. Hark!
now they play "hop scotch" along the extremities.
You give a sudden brush with
your hand; but you hit nothing. Now they
commence a tramp up, up, up! it is no longer
endurable. Out of bed, off comes the night-
dress, turned wrong-side-out. In the greatest
apparent rage at the harmless piece of cotton,
you thrash it most vigorously against imaginary chairs, get into it again, lift up the sheets
and go through the same pantomime against
bed-posts and foot-boards, which exist only in
your memory of things, in an entirely past
epoch of your life's history. Now they are
spread anew over the no longer unsuspected
bed. The sleepy little Miss Alice is packed
in after having received a thorough brushing,
of which she takes cognizance only in broken
dreams. You lay yourself away wearily — oh,
so wearily — after a whole week's travel, and
no true interval of rest, *hoping* to get asleep
before you are again taken possession of.
What a futile hope. Here they come like a
herd of homœopathic buffaloes, as if by a pre-
concerted signal, making head-quarters on the
open prairie between the high bluffs of your

shoulder-blades—nice, snug, table-land that—and "catch me if you can" seems to be the taunt with which they set up anew their night's banquet at your expense.

After all, it is not so much what these "varmints" take, as the manner in which they *do it*, that we rebel at. Commend me to a bold, pharisaical mosquito, who not only sounds his horn before him but, sipping once for all a sufficiency of blood, which the poorest of us can well enough spare, settles off upon a wall or curtain, content to rest and let others rest, till he feels the want of another meal: a sort of "Robin Hood" robber is this gentleman. While the Messrs. Flea and company are veritable "squatters" on "hitherto unoccupied territory," ostensibly for the "benefit of every race under heaven;" but really and truly for self-aggrandizement and gain.

With the early morning, we laugh at the type of us emigrants, so plainly drawn in a pocket edition; while at the same time, falling back upon our rights, said to be somehow covered by the United States Constitution, we say, quite boldly, "Gentlemen, these 'claims' are already *preempted;* you will please move farther up the territory."

Our ablutions are of course of the most superficial kind. Good old Jacob has not yet arrived among the pilgrims; and the water for man and beast comes from dame Nature's kindness, in opening sundry little springs on the ravine slopes, in this city of a year. It will take years to dig wells. They are not the absolute necessity that houses are; and the wonder to me all the while is, what can they stone them with after they are dug? There is nothing here but lime-stone. And the water now is but lime-water, too hard for cleaning purposes.

The days are intensely hot; everybody looks wilted and dirty: how can it be otherwise? Ex-Governor Reeder arrived here to-day. He is a fine-looking man, rather stout, with grey hair, the mien and air of a gentleman, and of the Philadelphia stamp. The people here seem very enthusiastic about him, at which I am not at all surprised. He is a brave and noble-hearted man.

Every day brings fresh loads of emigrants, from almost every State in the Union. Many fine-looking men, and really handsome women, and often quite large families of children, too, arrive. They tarry at the hotel for a night or two, then spread away to homes commenced for them somewhere in this bewildering wide country. Meanwhile I go over to the cabin, to hasten the completion of the floor. The promise of a few boards is a mere myth. The mill has a spasmodic "fever and ague." Just when you most hope to receive boards from it in return for logs, a "chill" comes on. No work done to-day!

The "lad" and his mother walk up Massachusetts street, to select a stove. We take time to discuss the different varieties and different prices. We go over to the cabin, and, sitting upon the old blue chest, go into a "committee of the whole," on finances. The principal question is, How *little* can we sustain ourselves on? What *must* we have to use, in the way of implements? First, then, we must have a stove. The price, thirty-three dollars! is quite frightful; but it will bring many conveniences with it; a thought of much moment in beginning at the foundation of civilized house-keeping two thousand miles from the active, ever-inventive Yankee spirit, where a want is hardly expressed before some ingenious mechanic, with more time than money, and a strong desire to make money, produces the article your necessities, whether real or artificial, demand.

We go out again; the stove is purchased. Across the street, at a little "shake" shop, we see tubs and pails; we pass over and purchase two cheaply-made tubs, a pail and a broom, all amounting in price to nearly double what you pay at home; but they are among the *necessities*; our consciences are at ease. Madam takes the broom, the lad one side of the tubs, which she makes a level by placing her left hand in the handle on the other side. This is our promenade to the cabin. Now we suspend operations, while poor Typhoid receives the remnant of the day in some trifling attentions to her bodily wants. Verily she is a pattern of quiet patience, going through the routine of a fever where people come and go in a common public room; making no complaint nor unreasonable demand.

It is quite amusing to hear travellers make

excuse to leave the apartment, when in any way it comes out that it is "Typhoid," upon the lounge. Not everybody, but some, perhaps the largest proportion, are afraid. To-night there comes one to tarry for the night who carries in his mien the beauty of manly courage. How I wish for the power, my mother, of graphic delineation, so that this specimen might appear before you as he did to me. Somewhere in an old family bible, well worn with use and bearing a broken clasp upon one side, I have a distinct recollection of an engraving of one of the prophets. Often of a Sunday, in that old east room, where few people ever ventured (for it was the best room), I took the heavy bible from its place on the table between the windows into a chair, and with a child's curiosity, took a peep at those old pictures. No one ever explained them. They have all passed away from my memory with the exception of this grand old prophet. Even now I see the fine head, the majestic beard, the heavy masses of curling hair, the uplifted hand and upturned eyes, with the flowing robes! Once, a very few years since, and yet how long it seems! that picture came to me, up among the hills, whither, in summer, we all love to take flight. It was August, when nature works so effectually that she can afford to seem idle; when the stillness of every growing thing is equal to the great progress it is making towards its fullness; when the white rolling clouds skim over the deep blue sky in heavy, harmless profusion. From the tea-drinking of a farm-house, with those who were dearly beloved, we entered a by-road for a twilight ramble. The sunset was most magnificent. We stood in silence till it sank below a fine wood in the distance. Clouds of the most gorgeous colors followed in the train: then a space of that clear, warm blue which often is to be seen before twilight, and, hanging above it, a heavy white drapery. We turned to look. A cry of one note — an instinctive clasping of every hand. We stood before the prophet again! clearly cut from that fleecy cloud, of size colossal, yet grandly proportioned. O, that it should ever fade away! The prophet of my childhood, came to me again! Not a word was spoken till the picture merged itself in the masses of cloud. And, even to this day, there is to us who saw it a sudden thrill whenever we speak about it, always ending with the remark, "If we could only see it again!" No *actual* could, of course, ever equal those two pictures in memory's gallery. But here comes a smaller edition of the same thing, — not small, though; very large, measuring one man with another, — a great deal of clear white hair, and an answering white beard; forehead high and broad; eyes deep-set under shaggy brows, and of a piercing brightness; a figure more than six feet; a voice mellow as the softest bass. He sits by Typhoid and talks, without fear of any disease, as though he was her father and everybody's father. He tells her of the great sickness up in the territory, — how whole families are on their beds, in some instances, with no one to bring them a drop of water; the doors of their cabins standing open. They are helpless to defend themselves, or provide for the most trifling want. When he arose to go I stood up, too; he gave every one his hand, and passed out to sleep in his wagon, under a buffalo, with a canopy of sail-cloth. The grasp of his hand was a benediction. Whoever he may be, whatever place he may fill among men, in person and majestic manner, I "ne'er shall look upon his like again."

Sept. 25th. — Your trio of descendants, my dear mother, take possession of the cabin to-day. The trunks, four in number, are moved over; the boards constituting the floor are drawn close together in the centre of the room, so as to accommodate the cooking stove, which we are hourly expecting. Alice and myself are sewing up some sacks of coarse, unbleached cotton, to be filled with prairie hay and used as mattresses to our lounges, which we have the promise of to-night. We sit a while upon one trunk, then try another, hoping it may be more comfortable; then we mount the old blue chest; but we cannot, in either position, cheat ourselves into the belief that we find rest to our backs. This leads us into another "committee of the whole" upon the question of indulging in the luxury of chairs. We price them, but can find nothing cheaper than two dollars seventy-five cents for a most frightfully-painted wooden rocking-chair, and one dollar each for ordinary kitchen chairs, not enough easier to sit in than the changes of baggage to justify the expense.

Meanwhile, sewing at the sacks, we take a peep at the chinks and corners of the cabin. The day is intensely hot; flies are having a home-like frolic, up midway in the room, and number more than ever I saw in one room before. They do not, however, seem inclined to interfere with us, their happiness being complete in the warmth of the day and the merry roominess of the space between us and the rafters. Soon I see coming down the beam near me a cricket-looking body, only large as a half-dozen home crickets. I move suddenly, but say, very quietly, "Ned, what lodger is this?" He is intimately acquainted with them, for he points to quite a small army of them in another direction, and says, " Only crickets. Everything grows large in this country. They won't hurt you. Why, they lived here by right before we came." Verily the boy is more of a philosopher than his mother. Will she ever get rid of her fear of bugs?

Now comes the man with two narrow frames for beds, into which I have cords laced, after the manner of a bedstead, believing they will be softer than the bars of wood laid across. We get them in readiness; hunt out the two blankets and one pillow, which we brought along in a trunk for any emergency. The "Bay State shawls" are fastened up and turned into tapestry against the walls, back of the lounges. Two quilts of stripped-up dresses, done by your hand, dear mother, are brought from the chest, and with them sheets, too, with the New England clean-odor still in their folds! What nice little beds they seem, if they are but prairie grass. Now, just as we light a candle, comes a dried, mottled little man, with the stove. He is equal to what he undertakes, and soon puts it in the right place, with the long funnel peering out above the roof. He kindles a fire to make sure his work is well done, and squats himself upon the floor to watch the result, and *rest* himself. I stand with the candle in a Japan candlestick of curious pattern, having a tube for matches, a dinner-plate-like bottom, from the centre of which rises a spy-glass set of tubes, which push the candle up or down as may be desired. The little man warms his begrimed hands by the open stove-doors. What a picture we make in the fantastic grouping of fire-light and candle-light; bright, clean little beds, heavily-corded trunks, a pleasant child's face, the dark, barn-looking roof, into which we can only trace objects dimly and fitfully as the fire burns up brightly or fades through want of fuel; and, standing in the background, the carroty-haired youth, with gray clothes, and felt hat drawn down over his eyes. The little man seems loth to go. We want our supper, and *he* wants sympathy, and asks it, creeping closer to the fire, for the nights are damp. He must tell me, in tedious detail, how sick he has been in his shop, with no one to care for him; and, child-like, goes back to his native home in Ohio, tells me all his little troubles, and how he always told his mother, in his letters home, that his health was very good, it would make her so unhappy to hear anything else. Out into the darkness went the little man, with a pleasant " Good night" from those who gladly made a light supper, and put themselves into a night position.

How much like sleeping out doors it seemed!

the cabin so small and thin. Out on the main street there were all manner of discordant noises — loud and angry talking, with an occasional report of fire-arms; nearer, even close to the cotton door, were the tinkle of cow-bells and the lowing of cattle. I call to Ned to explain their uneasiness. He says, an ox was shot close by, yesterday, and the skin hangs not far distant upon a fence, around which the cattle paw the ground, and moan, after the fashion of an Irish "wake."

This is too novel a position to be wasted in sleep. The moon comes in through the cotton windows. I watch the mice (not less than a dozen) play over the bridge of a floor, race over our baggage, climb up our nice shawl curtains; and, growing strong with the necessity for it, I drive them away only when they come too near the quilt. Morning comes, with no bread for breakfast, and no bread-store or baker to fall back upon in such an emergency.

There is some Graham flour, so we will have some griddle cakes. But what can we make them up in? Our utensils consist of a wash-basin of tin, a tiny tea-pot, a mug, brought with the tea-pot in my basket, a very little tin pail, property of the boy house-keeper, but of quite questionable cleanness, and an iron spoon with part of the handle broken off. The pail and spoon are made clean. But there is no salt—nevertheless we manufacture the cakes without it in the little tin pail, with water, and a pinch of soda. Just here I gained a new idea. The water is very strongly impregnated with lime, making bread or cakes, without soda, quite light; some butter, which could be dipped with a spoon, was used for frying; and the lime-water cakes, made in a hopeless state of mind, were light and very palatable. Alice turned the tubs over, the smallest tub mounted upon the larger, and spread three plates upon it. She was in an amusing state of dismay when she discovered that there was no way of sitting round her new-fashioned table, without chairs. So we shook hands with the little tea-pot, having the mug for our tea cup, arranged upon the old blue chest, and made love to the cakes from plates settled carefully upon our laps. We now again went into the science of economy, counting over our fast diminishing store of gold, and the many things we must have; while there opened to the eyes which had travelled the longest and saddest road, a picture of a long, new winter, which gladly, most *gladly*, she would have turned away from.

Oct. 1st.—Susie, who has been poorly for several days, has now a serious fever upon her. I go every day to "smooth her up;" little Typhoid, still unable to go about, is taken up stairs into the same room with Susie. They manifest their distress, as well as their gratitude, in as different ways as possible. Typhoid is peace and patience itself; Susie keeps up a loud demonstration of her pains and wants. But she is very pleasant, too. I believe she is really much the sickest person; and am afraid there will be more sickness in that house.

Coming home, I find the man of whom we get our milk, at the door. This man I must tell you about. Just opposite my door, twenty rods distant, stands a cabin made of turf. The man who lives in it keeps a few cows, and sells their milk. He is rather a good-looking specimen of a man, and quite gracious in his manner. Report says he is a clergyman from Pennsylvania. At any rate, his mission here seems to be, to make money. He trusts no one for milk, but sells you so many little tickets, each counting for a quart of milk, at five cents per quart. So far, so good. Daisy kept the tickets, and, what was more difficult, hunted up some sort of a vessel to put the milk in. But to-night there was something on his mind, and after I came in, he said he must raise the price of milk to eight cents a quart. It seemed to me quite a lift, from five cents to eight, but as I was not responsible for his plans, and did not wish to chaffer with him, I simply said, "We will reduce our quantity then." Thinking it over afterwards, how important milk was to the children, I called a "council," to consider about the expediency of buying a cow. Edward accordingly looked around and priced cows. We could get a good cow, for this country, for twenty-five dollars; and with her a calf, which, we learn, is *always* used as a "decoy-duck" to bring the cow home. We made up our minds that a cow was a matter of necessity, and of course a piece of economy, and that we would take up the remainder of the tickets and then set up on our own account in the milk line. Meanwhile, sickness multiplies everywhere, and the heat is very oppressive. I mounted the second story of the little barn I told you of, to see some men who, I was told, were sick there. In my hand was a pitcher of gruel, with a cup over it, for the double purpose of a cover and to feed them from, and in my pocket a silver spoon. The first man had a very sore mouth from salivation; he could hardly speak, but his fever was entirely gone; indeed, he had been brought in from the country, and from some "claim" which he had taken up previous to his sickness. He was partly dressed, and I asked him to lay upon the other bed, while I made his more comfortable. He seemed very much surprised to see me at all, as well as at my request; but he obeyed. I "dressed," to use the Irish epithet, his bed as well as possible, went out and got a pitcher of fresh water, washed his face and hands, using a clean linen from my pocket for the purpose. "Now," I said, "You must eat; it will clear out that dreadful mouth to swallow this gruel." He seemed to doubt his ability to get it down; but was quite assured by my confidence, and, taking my direction, which always is, when the mouth or throat is sore, to drink from a cup or tumbler large swallows, without stopping, till the vessel is empty—he drained the cup, and held it out for more, which I gave him. How glad he looked! Now he spoke with comparative ease; and I helped him into the newly-made bed, quite refreshed.

I knocked at the next door, from which came a faint "Come." It was a sort of closet, opening from the other, hot as an oven, almost, and contained two narrow racks for beds; upon one of which a slight-built, young fellow lay, looking as though he was buried, so far as friends were concerned. He looked so young and slight, I could have cried over him, if it would have done anything towards making him bigger and more fit to fight out a destiny in Kansas. But I did not conclude it would; on the other hand, I had made up my mind previously, that water, as an application, could not injure any person or thing hereabouts. So, brushing up the young man's hair with my hands, I kneeled beside him and tried to rouse him. He did not notice me much, or indeed anything else, till I said, "You will feel refreshed if I bathe you." So, after this preliminary, I went through with his head, face, and arms; then took the spoon and fed him, as you would a child. He did not need much, and was too sick to take it if he had desired it. But after he was through, and I turned to go out, he threw his arms over his head, turned his face to the wall, and I heard him say: "I ain't been so happy this thirteen months; 'pears like my mother has come."

I crept out, down stairs, to the room below, where David was sick. He had his share of attention, and begged of me to come again— to which I replied, he should have his share of my spare time. I then went into the house to ask what provision had been made for the night. Phebe said John would lie down on a couch by David, and take care of him. David seemed almost too sick to be put off with anything less than a wide-awake watcher; but I did not like to interfere. Besides, John was sitting upon the sill of the "wen" door, close by me; the night was coming in damp, and it seemed to me that he did not look well. Phebe said, in answer to my question, that he was not; but John did not speak to me. I thought his manner very strange. I still thought of it after I came into my cabin, and could not feel easy about the night arrangement for the sick.

Without being at all "clever," according to the English definition of the word, I do not think any person ever had keener instincts than myself. I often account for it on the principle that no creature is made without some peculiar, personal power of safety, or monition of what course to pursue as a means to that end. Be that as it may, certain I am, my work was hastened in the morning so as to be ready early to go the rounds. Before they were completed, a messenger came for Edward to go out five miles, to a cabin where four men were "down" (to use the country expression) with chills and fever. It seemed a clear case of duty to let him go, for a few days at least, — provided he could secure Paine, his old chum, to guard us at night. This was readily promised by Paine; and Edward rolled up his buffalo, jumped into the wagon, and was off. My visit was thus retarded. But soon I was on hand, full of the foreshadowing of more sickness.

Poor Davie, and poor John, indeed. John

laid himself down at Davie's feet, so, as he said, Davie might *kick* at him and wake him, if he slept too soundly. Davie's fever is very severe. John sank into a dead sleep, which often precedes sickness, not to be aroused by the pressure of Davie's foot, but to writhe in convulsions of which he had no cognizance. I can hardly think of poor, honest and patient Davie's night in that little barn-manger, without getting into a fit myself — it seems so dreadful — suffering as he is, receiving no help himself, and seeing this large, stout man rolling upon his narrow bed, until at last he springs over upon the floor, bruising his nose and face, causing the blood to flow as though he was butchered outright. Now, when the excitement is too much for Davie, and the peril to John quite serious, some one of all the hard sleepers in those rooms wakes, gets up, and takes the matter in hand.

My visit finds Davie purple almost with fever, three men holding John so that he may not harm himself, and the room in the greatest confusion. John, it seems, cannot possibly live. My anxiety is to get Davie out of the room. I remember the two beds, one only of which was occupied by Sore Mouth, up stairs, and in less time than I take to write it out to you, Davie was carried up there. I go up and sit down between Sore Mouth and Davie, and talk pleasantly for a while, making a very free use of cold water. They both talk to me of their *mothers*. Verily woman is majestic to her children, whatever she may be to any other person. These men, with coarse, brown features, unshaven faces, uncut hair, large and brawny arms, rough and horny hands,— how, in this interval of repose from hard labor, their thoughts go back to their childhood's home! and the mothers who bore them were the strong ties still holding them there. This is the fine gold in their hard natures, and almost the only charm, except that of relieving human suffering, which made their sick rooms pleasant. Here we were, all strangers to each other,— they confiding in me, and I striving to shut out some of the painful portions of their condition by making other portions more prominent,— which were indeed sources of great comfort.

There is in *reality* no *romance* in a sick room, especially if one has no personal interest in the parties. The romance of disease exists only in beautiful engravings, never coming out of the frame: like pictures of charming children, who never have dirty faces, torn clothes, or an evident necessity for pocket-handkerchiefs, hair-brushes or fine-tooth combs; — so, in these places of pain, where, from the new and unfinished state of everything, comfort is not to be had, it is made pleasant to go and come only by remembering long sicknesses of my own — blessed gifts from heaven — wherein I learned how to suffer with those who suffer. Getting up to finish my round, and look in once more upon John, Sore Mouth says, sadly, "You have not been in this Territory long, if you had, you could not laugh so lightly." Poor fellow, he did not know that the laugh was designed to aid directly the operation of his medicine — thrown in as a part of his necessary medical attendance.

Again I went in to poor John. I tried to make him know me; but he was wholly unconscious, and so little like a human being I could not bear it, and, for the first time, this morning, I went into the ten-foot wen, sat down by the cooking-stove, and burst into tears. Phebe came and stood by me, weeping. Then it dawned upon me that she loved John, and was probably engaged to him. Meanwhile Typhoid came for me, to say that Mr. C—— had returned the night previous, very sick, and that the first person he asked for was myself. While I stood talking with her about it, I noticed for the first time a gentleman, to whom she immediately introduced me as Mr. ——, of Philadelphia. His name you will remember as one familiar to me—he having been recommended to me as a proper legal adviser, should I need one. But, now I have seen him, I am pleasantly reminded of your dear son-in-law, Mr. Andrews, to whom he bears a most striking resemblance. I have neither time nor heart now to talk with him; I tell him so—it is my way, you know—and then I go to see after Mr. C——.

He is in the chamber over the hotel parlor. I knock. He answers, "Come in." He is thrown upon a narrow bed, still dressed, just as he came in from his political travels through the Territory. In the room are two wide beds, occupied by Germans with their wives. The women have risen; the men are sick. From two more narrow beds the occupants are shaken out and gone. C—— seems more worn out than sick, and quite distracted with the confusion of his room. I ask him if he will go home with me. He says, "Oh yes, most gladly!" I rush down stairs and out at the door, to see if any carriages are standing about. While looking round, one drives up. I attack the owner of it, like a highway robber, asking very earnestly, not for his purse, but for *him* and his carriage, to take a sick man a few rods to a cabin. He looked at me very curiously; but when I said Mr. C—— must suffer much from any delay, as he was in want of immediate rest, the name seemed to electrify him; he drew his horse close to the hotel door, and I started for home to be in readiness for his arrival. I had, in fact, given the possibilities in the case no thought at all — my poor accommodations, want of bedding and every convenience. It was another of those instinctive acts, which are always pleasant afterwards for me to look at; not as being a part of myself, but because I attach to them what you, who are wise may consider as a fallacy, the conviction, always so pleasant, of not being alone; of having another *me,* beside this most disagreeable intractable me, who sometimes comes to my help, so that I may lay up some treasures, pleasant to overhaul when the mind is in repose and solitude.

The carriage arrived almost as soon as myself; and Mr. —— followed close upon it, to offer any assistance. The cabin, after all, did not look so very badly. It was swept up clean, and had a sort of cleaned-up aspect, notwithstanding the cotton-wood floor; which you must know is very much like the downy side of cotton-flannel, and when experimented on with Kansas soil, becomes quite a peculiar color to neat housekeepers, who have had but one idea hitherto of floors, viz: that they should be washed occasionally.

Mr. C—— is a slight-built person, delicate complexion, sandy hair, fine forehead, gentle, manly manner, and about twenty-seven years of age. Is a native of Charleston, South Carolina, has a wife and three children, and a most devoted mother; all now living in Baltimore. I take the place of his mother at once. I help him off with his extra clothes and his belt with pistols; the latter are loaded, and he asks me to please place them under his bed within reach. This, mother, is a *necessity* of the country; and sick as he is, the habit makes him ask for the safe deposit of his means of personal defence. I feel so glad I have one pillow here for him, and two of those large, heavy blankets, because on this narrow couch one blanket can be doubled so as to answer for two. Poor fellow, he simply remarks, "How good the bed feels," and is fast asleep. I unlock the blue chest and dig up from its capacious depths the old piano cover, out of which I create a drapery around the front side of the little bed. Little Daisy and myself creep round as quietly as the mice; and the poor worn man, just home from a tramp through this great world of territory, sleeping in wagons or under them, speaking to assembled settlers in the open plain and under the stars, with the damp ground to stand upon, has a chance, I hope, to sleep away the indications of long sickness. But no; when he sleeps even, there is a burning heat 'fusing itself through his frame. I bring another sort of couch, made up for the occasion, close to the stove, and lay myself away upon it. The night grows very cold, and the wind creeps in everywhere. I am in a perfect chill, and cannot get warm even by a large fire. Mr. C—— sleeps quite well, and the unnatural heat about him makes him insensible to the change of temperature. How I shiver, and remember all the poor who know no other way of passing their autumn nights or winter days, than in this forlorn chill. If my bedclothes were only here, how comfortable we all might be! Strange they are so delayed! P—— sleeps soundly over-head, with a few old quilts of his. Can I ever learn to make so hard a bed the place of rest, forgetfulness, or dreams? Ah, mother of mine, I do like a nice bed, and am quite homesick without it all the while. Though P—— *seems* comfortable, I cannot reconcile it to myself not to place him more according to my ideas of ease and rest.

Morning is met with gladness—for the days are still warm. Morning brings the Doctor, and he confirms my fears of a fever for Mr. C——. Now the cotton door is thronged with calls, to see or learn of my poor patient. At first, I hardly dare refuse admittance. But, as the case becomes more serious, I close the door upon all. Now, surely, this mother's son and wife's and children's solace and support, must be closely cared for.

I leave Alice to watch, while I make a short call on other sick folks. Davie seems to need me most. He says, if he could have me all the time for two or three days, he should surely be well. John is certainly better; he takes some notice of those about him. It seems wonderful indeed!

Edward has returned, leaving his men all better, and is quite tired out himself. He has found a cow, and we are enjoying the nice milk very much. Mr. C——'s fever is unabated, and he is very restless under it. He is, I find, quite an important person in the political circle of Kansas; and as there is a State convention called to meet in about two weeks, his progress towards recovery seems retarded by his anxiety to be able to take his seat.

I am beginning to get very tired; but I can not give up my post at all. Other sick people are getting on faster than Mr. C——.

I drop away from them, to hurry him along. Wise men of the nation come in shoals to to the door, to say how important he is to them; and to express thanks for my taking him in charge. I had not the least idea that he was of more consequence than Davie, or any other person, when I took him home. But I see very plainly his temperament will make it hard work to get him up rapidly. I must devote myself to him. Here I sit, mother; the cooking stove is at my right hand, my poor invalid at my left; on the stove-hearth, stands the last of grand-father's coffee cups, which he fancied so much for their generous size, and standing in it the spoon, bearing your name at full length. I wonder how many times I read it every day, scan each letter, measure the whole word, knitting the while, often with my eyes closed, from a soreness gathering into them for the want of sleep. Now I see the lips of the sick man move. I lift the nice old spoon to moisten them, and return it again to the cup. Down before me is a tin wash-basin, full of ice-water, and a napkin old and soft. It seems to mesmerize the heated features, by its softness and coolness. The eyelids cease to quiver; quietness is in the cabin; my portfolio is at hand and takes the place of the knitting work; *you* are in my thought and close by me, with your womanly wisdom. The pencil, however, has no fears in limning for you, and through you, for others. You will smooth the defects, take in at a glance the divided thoughts between the sick and the well, the discomfort of writing without a table or an easy posture, day or night, without change of ideas or condition, from the fifteen-feet square of cabin, in which, look up or down, you feel as though every utensil and every article of apparel had been suddenly stricken with spasms, or gone irrecoverably out of its place.

Oct. 10*th.* — Our milkman called to say there was a very sick man in his cabin, he would like me to come in and see what I thought of him. I asked if his wife was well; whereupon he said he had no family but this man, who had been sick some time, though not dangerously; but now he seemed worse, and he thought if I would stop with broth or gruel when I went by, it would do him good to share it. Of course I went.

The cabin is simply a roof, with a fire-place and entrance at one end and a window at the other. I was surprised on entering, to see how very clean and comfortable it looked within. The walls were covered with cotton cloth; the ground with a cotton carpet; on each side of the window a bed was fitted in, and upon one of them lay the sick-man. He was alone, and I was almost afraid to go close to him at first. So I poured out some chicken-broth, for he had no fever, and went to his bed with it in my hand, after having set the door wide open. — Mother, you need not tell anybody; but I am truly a very great coward when my mind is in repose.

Mr. H——'s hair was very gray, and turned back from his forehead; his face pale and deathly, but dirty for want of washing. He had a buffalo skin over him, and when asked if he was warm, answered distinctly, "Yes;" though it appeared at a glance, that his mind was worn to shreds. I think his mouth is very handsome; but there is something about the atmosphere of his presence which kept me wanting to run home. I said to myself, "What a fool you are, why don't you feed him? nobody can be good when they are hungry."

How much we talk about the wickedness of the poor. But it's of no use trying to make them better; no use to talk to them about their souls, till we wash, and feed, and clothe their bodies. The wants of the body are an unforgotten fact, ever present. But the broth will get cold; so I'll feed this sad old man, and go. I ask him to take it, presenting the spoon, and holding the mug in the palm of my hand, with the fingers brought up over it. I am thus particular, because of his remark, over which Mr. C. has laughed heartily, and perhaps you may. The broth seemed to suit; but all the while he kept looking at the mug, as I supposed. Presently he smiled, and then he looked as though he would cry, but said, with the faintest voice, and with quite an interval between each word, "I should like to know who it is that feeds me." I told him I was Edward's mother. But he did not understand, evidently. Indeed, everything I said seemed to break the chain of his own thoughts. Now he rallied again, and smiled; but his only remark while I stayed, was, " There is a great difference in hands." Once, before I put my hands to steep in lime-water, I should have considered it complimentary, now I was wholly at a loss how to take him. But I made up my mind that the milkman should wash him clean, and I would feed him; and I accomplished my purpose.

Now, Edward has to go for me, for I am very lame and tired. But I have received a blessing in the shape of a brother of Mr. C., Lieut. C. of Baltimore, an older man, and a most willing, as well as excellent nurse. He comes in fresh and strong; keeps the fire up all night; sleeps like a soldier, with one eye open, and upon the floor, ready at a moment. Mr. —— has been the most devoted of friends. I wish you knew him, Mother, he is so much like Mr. Andrews. The best rest I have had has been when he has taken my place.

Oct. 20*th.*—No news of my boxes yet, and the weather has become very cold. There never was such a wind as those rocky mountains send over the country. It rocks the cabin like a cradle; and we can hardly hear each other talk. I feel as though we must be blown into the river, or off over the prairie. I open my lips sometimes, to call out to the mountains to "shut up that door, and not to freeze us out entirely. Why, you are worse than the Missourians. They want to burn us out; and between you both, where shall we fetch up?" Cotton windows won't do this weather, so we put in glass ones. Mr. —— holds a candle in the evening, while Mr. P—— puts one in; and I keep a great shawl up as a screen between the sick and the draught. Now for a wooden door! It is among the "must haves." Now I make paste, and secure every pair of hands I can, to help paste up newspapers over the walls of the cabin.

For several days, another invalid, a young clerk from Boston, has come in to be fed. There is quite a breaking up of eating places; perhaps because of sickness. I am too much of a stranger to know, and too little given to asking questions to learn. This young man I pity very much. He has chills and fever upon him alternately; and has no regular home.

He sleeps in an office, where I called twice to see him. Now, he creeps out a little; but there never was any disease so fully *up to* and really *capable of*, taking the entire pith out of a man as this same chills and fever. I could not refuse the sad victim of such rough handling the blessing of a warm meal, at any hour of day or night. Now, if ever, it is hard upon me to do it heartily. I am so *cold*, COLD; it seems as though my blood was frozen. Neither day nor night have I been warm this week. But we must paper out the cold wind — colder than any known to the oldest inhabitant.

Little Daisy keeps in bed. She does not seem very sick. Perhaps 'tis the weather. My heart almost fails me; but it won't do; everybody will freeze if these papers are not put on, two or three thicknesses. One can have no idea how much good they do, till they live in a "shake" cabin. My paste is used up. Two bricks are on the top of the stove, heating, to place as sentinels at the feet of my patients, to keep the wind out. The Lieut. is on hand, cheerful, careful for us all. I am tired; and by the great fire which he has kin-

dled, my aching limbs seem quite disposed to
thaw. The day's work is over. He spreads his
buffalo over the back of the great rocking
chair, and bids me get well heated up before
bed time. Daisy sleeps; so does the boy up
over head. I think of my clerk only, just now,
anxiously. He did not come in for his "toast
and tea." My head lies easily against the
warm buffalo. The poor clerk seems, to the
almost dozing fancy, many, very many sick
men — resting in uneasy, crazy-looking beds,
and very many in a bed; in fact, each bed
seems a nest of rough, uncombed heads, with
burning cheeks and shaggy beards; while
hands, hard and sunburnt, reach after me; lips
move imploringly for me to moisten them. I
am hunting hopelessly — the awful hopeless-
ness of nightmare — for water, napkins, and
gruel. Oh, they will all die, and I can't help
them. I utter a cry, which startles even myself. My surprise is momentary, to find myself
in bed, with people watching carefully over
me. My mind slips out of the things they say
and do, into the states in which it has been
strained to the utmost for many days. Now,
the hurry is, to keep a poor forlorn woman

from freezing. My gray travelling dress is the first thing I put my hand to, and strip it into narrow ribbons, to tuck into the cracks about her bed. The excitement again gives vent to itself in mutterings, and broken words, waking me again to a sense of pain and sickness. Now reason comes back to me; and close to it, for a moment, I hear the flapping of the wings of despair. The *hub of the wheel is broken,* what will they do without me?

It is daylight. Mr. —— has just closed the door softly after him, and gone home to get a nap, after his night's watching. In the rocking-chair sits the good Lieutenant, sipping a cup of tea. Again the door opens, and Edward comes in with the milk. I lift the corner of my curtain and look over to see how the sick man is. He, too, is sipping tea. I'm sure he must be better. It makes me better to think he is. The quick ears of the Lieutenant hear me; he bobs his curling hair up above the chair, turns his honest, cheerful face round to me. "Tell me how many children you have," I asked. I believe he thought me out of my senses. But he answered me truly— "Four." "Then you can have no objections to my calling you 'Uncle Jeff,' for I am in my second childhood?" "Call me anything you please, so you only get well," was his reply.

Now it dawns upon me more fully, that I am sick. I beg to get up. I beg, too, if I cannot get up, that they will not tell you. Indeed, I'm quite sure I can write you myself in a few days; and, like my sick people over the way, I am ready to speak falsely almost, rather than you shall hear how badly-off we are. I can form no idea of the time I have been laid aside. By the pain and weariness, and the dead level of thought, it seems as though time moved sluggishly, and would never end. How powerless we all lie here; full of the strange fancies of sick people; longing for something quite impossible to obtain; or if obtained, quite unsuitable for us to have.

But O! the water — the water, gushing down the stony streams of dear New England! — never failing in the old mossy-stoned wells — how our lips parch for some of it! how our thoughts dwell upon its coolness, abundance, and sparkling clearness, until, in feverish dreams, we seem to reach and taste it! How we go back, always to pleasant home-looking chambers, — the glare of light subdued by green blinds without, and clean curtains within. How our outraged sense of harmony and good taste lingers over the conveniences, as well as decorations belonging to a past life, from which, by a strange and new turning of the wheel of destiny, we seem to be entirely and forever banished.

The habits of years, how strong they become! The tones of a piano, even though it were but the simple practice of a new learner, how gratefully it would break upon our ears! The tones of a bell, telling the hour of day or night, calling to church, or tolling a funeral knell — the distant rumble, the nearer whirl, and still more near shrill whistle of the steam engine, — how, as never before, would they make us feel not quite banished from the earth!

Now "Uncle Jeff" comes to me with tea, and the promise of a place by the fire tomorrow, should the weather moderate. He tells me, too, of a grand hunt which is to come off in a week, the game to be served up in the dining-room of the yet-unfinished hotel. He presents me an invitation to the supper, and is quite sure we shall all be well enough to attend. The week rolls round: the game hunt is very successful; birds, turkeys, ducks, squirrels, rabbits, and *blackbirds*, almost without number, are brought in to the committee of superintendence. The tables are well laid, and decorated with fancy cooking, got up under the skilful supervision of a lady from Worcester. A pie made entirely of blackbirds is an object of general interest. Whether there were the proper nursery number, of "four-and-twenty blackbirds baked in one pie," I am not able to learn. But the party was very successful, and most satisfactory to a larger number of people than ever before met for amusement in this territory — many of the guests coming thirty-five miles. The good "Uncle Jeff" does not forget those at the cabin, whose appetites have outgrown "toast and tea," but brings in a dish which, if not a portion of *the* blackbirds, is quite palatable enough to satisfy even more particular people than those he serves so kindly.

By way of experiment upon the returned strength of our nervès, we have had two shelves put up for the dishes, and a floor spread over the whole of the chamber. It was really quite a test of strength, and the nailing down of the floor was set aside. Now comes a heavy rain. How dull and dark everything seems, and how the rain beats against this cabin, as though it had some especial spite to vent. By way of pastime, we open the great seal-skin trunk, where, in the folds of sheets, pillow-cases, and napkins, are smuggled away bits of choice China,—choice, not only for its intrinsic value, but from long association. I believe we are all startled to find how large a portion of it is crushed in pieces. As it settles down in my lap from the folds of the linen, so utterly ruined, I scatter it through the cracks of the floor, where the mice carry on their domestic arrangements. Now we reckon up that which remains perfect and find we shall have enough for our own use, and quite as much as the shelves will hold. Five of your beautiful cups and four saucers, three of Miss Sallie C——'s cups, only, and seven saucers, out of a dozen. What would the precise old lady say, could she look down into the mice-territory under this cabin, where glisten the fragments of what adorned her table so many years? Two tumblers we find whole, one saltcellar, and plenty of plates.

How rich we feel! and how we begin to look forward, as well as backward, to a condition of civilized housekeeping! And how, too, my dear mother, the olden-time housekeeping comes to me, as a Sabbath-rest time, which will by some process, come round to me again,—when you will preside, as of old, and this *me* keep house within the circle of your atmosphere. Till then, give your blessing to your daughter.

H. A. R.

THE MISSOURI INVASION.

November 4th, 1855.

My Dear Mother:—This is the first Sabbath in November, and we are having a pouring, beating, east-wind rain,— quite an unusual quarter from which to "scare-up" a rain, or a wind even, in this region of the world. Our roof does not leak; but the east side of the cabin is its weak side. The shakes are not so closely packed; and the newspapers which we pasted on so carefully are loosening with the united action of wind and rain. I am already sliding off the papers, scattered in such profusion by Mr. C——'s friends about him, so as to have some to fall back upon when the sun comes out again, and the wind, getting weary, falls asleep. The inmates of the cabin are all dressed to-day. Night-gowns have rolled themselves up meekly and vanished under imaginary pillows. The contents of the dressing-gown, packed into the great rocking-chair, with giddy head and shaking hand, strives to get up a magnetic grasp of your hand and a breath of the repose which, ever and always, hovers over the room where my mother lives.

I could not write any more yesterday. We had a great many callers, gentlemen to see Mr. C——, and we all grew too weary to make ourselves agreeable, either by talking or writing. E. has been in quite early this morning to attend to poor Mr. Hadley. From E.'s account, I think he must be near the last of his journey. I hoped in a day or two to go to see him, he is so very near. But now, while I write, there comes a tap at the door, which (we all being invalids), I answer, with a cheerful " Come." The door is opened by a young lad about E.'s age; a stranger. He asks, " Is this Mrs. R.?" To which I respond, " Yes." He steps in, bringing a clean shirt in his hand, and, laying it upon my lap, asks if I will "Please put buttons to it, as it is wanted for Mr. Hadley's shroud." The work-basket is lifted down from a nail on the beam over my head; and, while I select the proper buttons, the young man tells me he was alone with the dying man, and that he lived but a few moments after E. came away. And now I sit here seeing the men of years, who should not have left these young hands to the sad work of closing dying eyes, go to prepare the poor, worn-out body for its safe and last repose.

Poor Hadley! and poor everybody who comes away from home to die among strangers. I am glad he had so little consciousness, and I give thanks that heaven is as easily reached from Kansas as from any other point under the sun. I never, in feeding the poor creature, could forget that somewhere, perhaps, he had a mother, or a wife, or a daughter, whose heart would wither from never knowing his final end. So long as I have known him, he has never had clearness of mind sufficient to tell his own story.

Now the picture changes again. The door opens to admit Grove L——, the Governor's private secretary. He is always welcome, with his pleasant smile, showing a wealth of teeth, and his ringing voice, full of the elements of music. He throws off his blanket, and says he is "bound to stay." I look at him with a bewildering stare, which he answers back by saying he is sick, and his death, (should he fail to impress the necessity on his part, and the *duty* on mine) must be inevitable. I point up to the loft, as the only resort at night. He gives a spring up the bars, looks about, and comes down quite satisfied.

At night he brings his buffalo, chair, and some books. The great chair is drawn near enough to the stove to tend the toasting-forks, and the bread, nicely browned, is passed from one to another, till those who drink milk, and those who content themselves with Kansas tea, are all supplied. Night settles down upon us. The pinched and faded cheeks of little Alice are the first to be laid away behind the piano cover,—which indeed makes a nice bedroom of that corner of the cabin. Then Mr. C——, broken to the merest wreck of manhood by his protracted and exciting sickness, is established in the warm corner near the stove. Dressing-gown hangs itself, with tall dignity, upon a nail, while night-gowns have their turn. The cabin is still. Good Uncle Jeff has taken care for us all, and at last drawn out his pillow of wood, rolled himself up in his buffalo, and is sleeping, as the honest soul always should, the even sleep of childhood.

There is peace in the cabin, my dear mother. "The angels of the Lord encamp around about those who fear him." Far off across the river, in my wakefulness, I hear the whoop of the Indian, or the echo of a rifle; or quite as often, the quarrelling sound of angry and hungry wolves. We accustom ourselves to new and disagreeable things with wonderful facility. The mouse, that I have just ordered off my bed, is no longer an object of terror, but simply a disagreeable *fact*, such as one meets with, in some form, every day of one's life.

I now calculate the amount necessary for breakfast, for the fastidious little company in the cabin; remember with relief the large loaf of light bread not yet encroached upon; the beef, from which the best steak can be cut, if needed; the corn-cake which can be stirred in a moment if begged for; and sleep, so coveted, comes in and puts out my lamp.

Nov. 8th. — We are having a very soft air, and the most charming weather: no frosts, and as warm as your June. It gives no strength to invalids, however, and they get sad under it. There is but little to interest minds weakened by long disease. No pleasant suites of rooms to walk through; no book-shelves to look over, or books of plates, to beguile the time hanging so heavily; no seats out doors to sit upon and chat; no daily mail to stir one's blood, when the announcement is, that the "mail is open."

But here comes Typhoid, tall beyond any woman I ever saw. An Indian head and hair, and a fine set of teeth. She has a brown veil tied under her chin, and a shawl thrown about her person. We always welcome Typhoid. She comes with an earnest message this time. One of the party who arrived from the East, that bitter cold week, has been there sick ever since; no one has taken particular care of him, and now the Doctor pronounces his disease, which is Congestion of the Lungs, so she said, incurable. Could I go over and see him? To be sure I would if possible. The hood is drawn on, the dressing gown exchanged for the dark print like yours, my shawl twisted tightly, by the zealous boy, around me, and with him for a body-guard, we start out.

We prefer to go into the main street, so long unseen, and mark the progress of things. Every step or two I stop and take an observation and give vent to an emotion of surprise that *so much* is doing. A city, just one year old, working up so many nice little stone dwelling-houses and more ambitious stores! A hotel, too, with its windows all glazed, and its black-walnut doors shining with the polish of oil! I have to scramble over great piles of sand, and heaps of the homesick-looking limestone. All sorts of merchantable matters hang and lie about all sorts of curious looking shops. Plenty of Missouri market-wagons stand up and down the street. "Ned," said I, "has anybody dug a well?" "Have n't heard," was the boy's reply. When shall the want of water be met? Will this generation produce no "Jacob," who has philanthropy enough to do so praisworthy an act? I'm sure he would deserve to have for his epitaph those concise words: "He digged a well."

But here we are at the door of the sick man. He is in the chamber we occupied during our first week in Kansas — a thin, woman-featured face; light hair in profusion, clammy with perspiration; not more than twenty-three years old. To my inquiries, he said with politeness, he was very well, " a little crowded, just a little; it's choking-like to be crowded;" and he looked about the room. "What crowds you?" I said. He shook his head and said: "Beds, Beds — very little room — great many beds!"

"To wet his mouth and smooth the clothes was all that could be done; and we came away from him. He has a brother somewhere in the territory; but, so far, no clue whereby to find him has been discovered. If we could only borrow a telegraph wire from you who are so rich in means and appliances of intercommunication, or an express-train, just for one day, then this poor youth should receive the care and love of his brother. What can I do for him? is the question unanswered, as we take a cross-way home, no longer cognizant of the outer working of poor human hands upon mortar, lime-stone and timber. This poor youth, " crowded," as he says; looking with dim and wistful eyes over his shoulder, with the weight on his breaking faculties of crowding beds in his sick-room, which should be so orderly and peaceful. What has the poor fellow done, that thus in his last hours he should be so thrust out of home and place? It is so pleasant to give the departing, the outward semblance of a Saturday-evening readiness and peace, in the arrangements of their rooms and persons, so that "*early*," to one so weary, "ere the day begins to dawn," the sweet repose of the Sabbath may be entered upon by anticipation.

William Dillon, what can I do for thee? poor, tired, dying emigrant! "*Crowded!*" crowded indeed! I come home to *think* of this new type of suffering. "If his brother — if his brother could only be found!" I say, as in my powerlessness I come in to the care of my own slowly-recovering invalids. I excite their sympathies by telling them the story of tired, crowded, dying William Dillon, of Michigan. They forget their own miserable feelings, in view of his more desolate condition, and begin to recount the riches of the cabin.

Nov. 10*th.* — You will be glad with me, my

dear mother, when I announce the sudden arrival of Mr. Dillon. Do you remember a favorite expression of grandmother, that "Man's *extremity* is God's *opportunity!*" No one here knew where Mr. Dillon went. The two brothers arrived here as travellers, with a crowd of emigrants, in a most severe "spell" of weather. William, being slightly unwell, remained; the other went his way. Three weeks passed. People came and went again from the little hotel; the reserved and quiet sick man attracted no one to him enough to communicate his history; so that, when he became very much worse and his mind broke down, he could only tell what was known before, that he had an elder brother who went up further into the Territory. To-day this brother suddenly appeared. He is wholly overcome to find his brother so low. Says he had an impression so strong that his cold had become a serious sickness, that he could not remain where he was, at St. Joseph's, and came back to learn the truth. William recognized him, and seemed to rally so much that even the physician thought he might recover. But it was only the sudden light and warmth stirred by the emotion of family affection, giving a glow to brighten his last hours. At twelve he ate quite freely from the hand of his brother, and talked pleasantly. At five he closed his eyes peacefully, to open them on scenes where he will never "chill" any more, or feel that smothering crowdedness he so significantly expressed in his manner, when he looked at the number of beds about him.

It seems to me now, as though it was not so much the *things* there were about him, as the discordant, unsympathizing atmosphere, which would most naturally arise from the ever-shifting occupants of those travellers' berths.

Nov. 15th. — Our life is a November day, tearful, lowering, and uncertain; promising faintly, and never renewing earnestly our faith in a clean and genial sky. My little Alice is not so well. It does not seem to be the result of a cold, or in any way a relapse. There is an entire change of symptoms. For three weeks past she has simply been laid aside with some fever. She has had bright red cheeks a portion of the day, and no appetite, together with a total loss of her usual animation. The getting up was, like her going down, not very decided; but she went out to look after her pets with some of her former interest. I do not think I have ever told you about a dog which came here quite of his own accord. One day a Missourian called with his market-cart, to sell apples and potatoes. He had a fine dog with him, which, as he was hot, walked into the next cabin, which was quite unfinished, and laid down to sleep. That cabin is owned by a wicked-looking man from Alabama, and occupied by another fellow of much less capacity, from Illinois. The last-mentioned man was the one who came and finished out the floor, which I think I wrote you about. This man took possession of the dog till Missouri had gone home; or, to use his own words, he "stole him." The dog would not, however, acknowledge him as master; but, as soon as he was turned out, came and joined himself to Alice. It seemed a genuine *first love* on both sides. Wherever she went, he followed; and at night laid himself down close to the cabin door of cloth, and kept faithful watch till morning. No creature could come near without his giving the alarm, in a deep and terrible growl. He is very large, marked from nose to the end of his tail in rings of two shades of tan color, most beautifully shaded. So we gave him the name of "Tiger."

In process of time, Alabama came to live with Illinois; and as they were in the habit of slaughtering cattle, he took up Tiger, and tied him near the meat, to protect it. All night long the poor fellow howled so as to disturb the whole house. The greatest cruelty was shown to the dog, because he would not stay with them; as though there was a royal road along which love and devotion could be driven! Ten days since, Alabama turned himself east as far as the old home of Illinois, they having made an exchange of some property; and our loving, beautiful, brave Tiger was tied into the wagon and transported also. Alice has never talked about him, since he was hopelessly gone. But now my little mountain daisy is very sick; she cannot turn herself in bed; and I watch by her, feeling as though I had brought her into this strange country to wither and die! In her fever-turns, her mind wanders back to old and pleasanter objects, and she says continually, "Please take me home; oh, I want to go so much!" At times, it seems quite impossible for her to recover; but then, again, she brightens up, seems more comfortable, and the utter impossibility to conceive of myself trudging along in the world without her, gives me temporary faith to believe that she will recover.

For two months we have slept upon straw, with our skirts folded at night, to make pillows, and every garment within reach spread about us, to keep off the piercing winds, which, from the non-arrival of our boxes, put our lives in peril.

There is one impression to which my friends, in writing, often allude: it is this—that I looked too much on the bright side of Kansas life, and should thus suffer more in the reality. Mother, I don't believe YOU see me in that light. There must be a defect in me, whereby I sometimes give an impression quite opposite to what I intend. I suppose, if I was going to have a limb amputated, instead of looking forlorn, and uttering sighs and moans, I should be more likely to joke and laugh over the matter; quite as much to keep up my own spirits, as those who might chance to be with me. *You* would understand, from instinct, that it was simply one way of "putting the best foot forward."

How strange it is, to be sitting here, holding in my hand a pen, wherewith I relieve myself by saying anything I please to you; laying aside, very often, this same pen, which seems to my spirit to actually touch you, that I may moisten the parched lips lying close by my side, powerless to do anything more than accept the cooling draught. The kind physician comes in often and sits awhile; but gives no medicine. She has taken nothing but the drops of water for nine days; and all her requests are, "Please take me home; please take me home." Mr. C——, slowly recovering, sits down by her, and promises to take her home before Christmas. She believes in him. Man is ever a gospel to woman from her earliest youth. But how shall he redeem his promise?

Nov. 21*st*. — My dear mother, to-day's mail brought your invaluable letter, which has been read very often, in curious little scraps of time;

coming out from my pocket while waiting for the boiling of the tea-kettle, or between the turnings of the toasting bread, the frying griddle-cakes, the handing up a hot meal from the fire to the hungry sitters around the table, or the waiting upon the faded blossom stretched away in the tented corner—now giving hope of a slow return to health, pleading no longer simply for water, but bread, too. Poor little blossom, what wanted I for thee here, that you are coming again upon the feverish track, where all wear out a weary or disastrous life? She has taken your little note and read it very carefully. Now she talks much about you, and your nice room, and of all the family. What strong affections she has! what shall we do with them?

You will be glad to hear that Mr. C—— is sufficiently recovered to go up into the Territory. If I supposed it would interest you half as much to hear of the progress of State matters, as I flatter myself it does to hear about our domestic arrangements, I'm sure I would pay more attention to all that is going on outside the cabin.

Since the fall elections Missourians have

kept very quiet, coming up here to supply us with plenty of very fine apples, potatoes, poor butter, and ordinary flour; making quite a thriving business out of it, and, as I have supposed, settling down into the conclusion which we all do, when we learn to know people — that they are better than we expected. Last week, however, a man living about six miles from here upon a claim, while walking towards a blacksmith's shop, was shot down by a party of Missourians, without any provocation. The border Missourians are a horseback people; always off somewhere; drink a great deal of whiskey, and are quite reckless of human life. There is no necessity for hard work to those who have long lived in this country, the earth yields so very abundantly. They ride fine horses, and are strong, vigorous-looking animals themselves. To shoot a man is not much more than to shoot a buck. After killing this poor Yankee, they stood around him till they saw a man approach, and then rode deliberately away. He who first came to the dying man went immediately to Mr. Branscome's, where the man had boarded. The two carried the body home. Nothing was done about it, any way, to my knowledge. This week, on Tuesday night, some one knocked at Branscome's cabin-door. He asked, "Who is there?" The reply was, "A friend." This again was replied to with a cheerful "Come in, then," though it was in the night-time, after people had retired. Immediately the little cabin was filled with armed men; the foremost one, going close to the bed, presented a loaded pistol to the head of Branscome, commanding him to rise and dress quickly, for he was a prisoner. Of course, the man did as he was commanded; left his poor wife, and was mounted upon a horse found ready for him by the party. Meanwhile the party, consisting of less than twenty, were full of expressions of regret that no "Yankees" were there to have some fun with. Officer Jones and his men took first one road, then another. Branscome became fully persuaded that his days were numbered, but sat quietly upon his horse, knowing resistance was quite in vain. It was not long before the oft-expressed wish of the Missourians was most singularly gratified. A portion of the Wakarusa militia company had been over to see about the murdered man, and were riding home quietly, by the usual route, when they met the Missourians, asked "Who goes?" and were answered, "We have a prisoner."

"Who is it?"

"Mr. Branscome."

The captain of the company said, "Mr. Branscome, ride out here." Mr. Branscome rode forward — the sheriff protesting against the order, but refusing to give any reason for the arrest; at the same time swearing he would shoot him if he moved. Mr. Abbot then replied, "We are all armed, and shall take Mr. Branscome into our ranks." He then ordered him off the horse, if it was not his own. Branscome immediately dismounted. Capt. Abbot commanded him to fall into his ranks and "march." The party from Missouri, wholly discomfited, and having had quite enough of "fun" with the Yankees, offered no farther resistance.

In the short hours of the night, the sound of a drum came from afar to my wakeful ears, nearer and nearer, but still not like the rapid call of a company together. It was simply one beat, then a pause. The young man who calls the drum-roll was asleep in the loft over my head. I was not kept long in suspense, for he "beat" quite early, to call a citizens' meeting. Lawrence was up and dressed *early*, and as wide awake as his ancestors of Seventy-six.

The prisoner, and those who came to the rescue, were called upon to state the facts, after which my two young friends, Grove L—— and M. F. C——, made most effective speeches. I learn that they did themselves much credit.

I dare say you may have heard Lawrence spoken of as an ultra, headstrong young sprig, who is always treading upon his neighbors' corns, or otherwise exciting to a fuss. But there never was a greater mistake. Lawrence is a hard-working, mind-his-own-business, money-loving fellow. If he hits your toes, it is not from design, but because his boots are stiff and clumsy and his manner anything but graceful or fascinating. Lawrence has seen hard times in his youth; has been laughed at by his more prosperous neighbors, till the ragged urchin made a bad matter worse by wasting some considerable emotion upon the subject; looked round fearfully and almost imploringly, to see if "Uncle Sam," or some other relative, would not give a hand to help him out on better footing. But Uncle Sam has grown old, gouty, and unfeeling. Much prosperity and too high living puts him to nodding in his chair. Alas for his far-off frontier children, when they have only him to look to! And New England, dear New England, the very dust of which is most precious to Lawrence! the whir of her looms, the rattle of her mills, the steam of her numberless engines, make such a noise that poor, awkward Lawrence's cry for help is quite unheeded, except, perhaps, in the passing of a few well-sounding resolutions, which remind one of champagne, long exposed to the air, from which the life and sparkle is gone forever.

Lawrence sits down in his cabin. His floor is of cotton-wood, rough and unwashed; his venison and beef hang upon the wall; his vegetables, in baskets over his head. Lawrence listens, with ears sharpened by intense longing, for sympathy and aid where nature's great heart prompts him to look for it,— from his kin. He reads how New England thrusts her hand into well-filled pockets, and, with self-gratulation, not to say pharasaical pride, takes out thousands to send to the sick at Norfolk, who are surrounded with cities rolling in wealth, where a sacrifice of any trifling pleasure would supply many such sorely tried and afflicted cities with any amount of assistance. Lawrence lifts his eyes from the cotton-board floor, with a new light in them. He thinks of all his suffering brothers and sisters, from this to the Rocky Mountains, sick and in want of all things,— no nurses, no water, no comfortable shelter, no pleasant sounds of church-bells, or busy marts of thrifty trade, to bring back receding life, and, more than all, no ever-returning word of cheer and remembrance from the home that was first and most dear; and, as he reflects, Lawrence is startled by the sound of violence within his own precincts. He sat down a homesick, disheartened youth. He had asked help from the agent of his great uncle at Washington, without success. Now the hour for action has come, and he rises, passes out of his cabin, armed like a man, ready to defend his rights like a man,— and may Heaven speed the RIGHT!

My dear mother, this is Saturday evening.

I am alone in the cabin with the faded Daisy. She has been up for the first time to-day, and borne her weight by taking hold of different objects to support her. Now she gladly takes her place again upon her couch, close by the stove, and sleeps quietly. Her mind is still very weak and child-like;—child-like, to be sure, it always is; and the exciting condition of the town, our own wakeful nights, do not affect her with any emotion of fear. How strange it will seem to you to hear that I have loaded pistols and a bowie-knife upon my table at night, three of Sharp's rifles, loaded, standing in the room, and two or three men in the cabin beside Edward, except when it is their turn to keep guard through the little town. All the week every preparation has been made for our defence; and everybody is worn with want of sleep.

The Missourians have taken awful oaths to destroy this Yankee town, and a price is set upon the heads of some of our most honored citizens. Already they have assembled to the number of two hundred at Franklin, a little town south of us, and many more at Douglas, a village farther up the river. They are moving with great secretiveness; but when was a Yankee "caught napping," in the faintest prospect of danger?

Last night our watch were cheered by the arrival of fifteen armed men from Ottoman Creek, who heard of the threatened danger and travelled till midnight to offer their aid. And to-day twice that number marched in with a flag, from Palmyra, another settlement fifteen miles from this. Paschal Fish, too, who lives ten miles nearer Missouri than Lawrence, has heard the rumors, watched with his Indian keenness the Missourian movement, mounted his pony, ridden up to see us, and offered to muster out some of his tribe, to be on the spot to-morrow. The Wyandott tribe have sent in one of their number to offer assistance, which is most thankfully accepted.

Your Thanksgiving evening, while you were, I am sure, talking and thinking of us, I sat here alone, watching by Alice, pale and faint, with the sounds of fire-arms coming every few moments from some direction. Standing at my door, C———'s little black pony, saddled, ready for any moment, has kept me company all the week. He puts his nose against me in the most kindly manner every time I have occasion to go out; and we talk long talks together, he always seeming to end the matter by saying, "Keep heart, I can take you anywhere you wish to go."

To-night everybody is at the hall. My orders are, if fire-arms sound like battle, to place Alice and myself as near the floor as possible, and be well covered with blankets. We already have one bullet in the wall, and, since that, one struck the "shakes" close by the bed's head and glanced off. Now, for the first time, I begin to take an interest in Lawrence, as a city; and, prospectively, her destiny is almost as my own. How well her men bear themselves, in the settlement of every question which is pressed upon them, now so important as a matter of national history. I can but hear and know of their plans, because Lieut. C—— and Grove L—— are a part of our family, and are among the most active workers. They come in to talk, consult with others, and write, if need be. Sometimes things assume a most amusing aspect; as when, after a serious charge to be sure and wake them up if the drum beats,

I, hardly daring to close my eyes, at last, half-asleep, hearing the most fiendish outcry ever borne upon the moon-lit night air, call aloud, "Wake up, quickly! there is trouble of some kind, for nothing but a Missourian could utter such sounds this side of the infernal regions!" and the cabin is astir in an instant,— only to laugh at me, because the unearthly sounds are only those of a party of wolves taking a survey of the city at midnight.

Dec. 5th. — Mother of mine, I can hardly settle down to the details of our own matters. Everything over the town, and every rumor borne in to us from outside of it, is more and more dark and fearful. We now have an armed force of five hundred men, who are under the command of Dr. Robinson, now commander-in-chief, and Col. Lane, both of whom have had experience in actual battle, in Mexico and California. Out of my south window I can see them drilling; far off it is, on the prairie; but you know we have a wide scope of observation. There is not a tree anywhere to be seen; and, as I look, the expected Indian tribe rides in, single file, at full gallop.

How well they ride! It is difficult to imagine them man and horse. They seem to be one, so closely does each rider cling to the well-trained animal he loves so well and passes so much of his life with.

The sun is just putting on his night-cap, and smiles back on the terraced hills ere he sinks to rest. Now the militia march back into the little town which they have come to defend. Alice is asleep; Ned busy at the door. I put on my hood and slip across to a nearer point, that I may see better. It is the first time out doors since she sickened; or rather, since I went to see William Dillon. I enter the little hotel where Dillon died. The landlady takes me by both hands, with a pocket-full of questions, drawn out one after another in quick succession, giving me no time to answer. Her gentle heart is fluttered with fear and kindness, too! She does not want anybody hurt, and she does not want her house torn down over her head. She believes, still holding my hands, I can settle the matter for her; which is in a measure done by pleasant jokes, a hearty laugh at her fears (hypocrite that I am, holding at the same moment my own troubled and faint heart,) and, last of all, by reference to the better guidance which does not forget or forsake us in the hour of need, but, if trusted, keeps us in the hollow of His hand, and guides us with His eye. We draw close to the window as the soldiers pass by to the tune played long, long ago by the military band in our native village, far off from this; but not farther than this woman who writes to you is from the little girl who used to hang out of her bed-room window and listen to the march, believing it the finest music in the world.—Mother, how fast I am catching up to you! almost as old now—don't you see? We will live together when we are old, won't we? But what a long line of men it is! Not noisy; and there is no rabble of boys at the roadsides. Boys there are in the ranks; but the soberness of manhood is upon them, and the determination of "Seventy-six" in their step. The blood warms in my veins as I look. The commander and his aids (one of whom is Grove L——, as brave and noble a heart as ever strode a horse for battle) look well. And now,—yes, it can be no other,—passes the prophet-head and flowing beard. I accept it as a good omen, slip out of the door in the side of the "*wen*," and am at home in a moment. L—— is close upon my path, with another officer, by the name of Deitzler. C—— is sitting with Alice; Ned is cutting up a pumpkin for the cow's supper. But my presence scares them all up, with the remark, "Shall we have any supper?" "To be sure you shall have some supper, in fifteen minutes." My tea-kettle is in my hand as I speak, and filled and placed in the stove before I take off my hood, a pan of biscuits thrust into the oven as I unpin it, and, when it is laid aside with my shawl, I uncover my wash-boiler, and draw up from its capacious depths a piece of corned beef. This is cut thin, and a plate of butter and a sheet of gingerbread are brought out, and your cups are spread out on the black-walnut board. The tea-pot is steaming on the top of the stove, and a pot of cocoa. My fifteen minutes are not out; but the family are ready and the officers in haste. There is to be a council of war at seven o'clock; and they say every token indicates action.

Teams coming up from Kansas City to-day, loaded with freight for our merchants, have been stopped by the mob tented near Franklin, and looked over; all bags of powder and other ammunition taken out, receipted for, and the teams allowed to go on; and teams of provision — apples, flour, and potatoes, stopped entirely. You see, mother, Lawrence is a very forbearing fellow, not to go down to Franklin and drive the brutes home about their business. But our people all say, we prepare for a *defensive* war, not an aggressive one.

So, then, supper is over. L—— takes up his constant companions, his belt with pistols and his rifle; he lingers in the cabin-door for a moment, comes back to say "good night; everybody sleeps on their arms to-night in the hall."

"Take your buffalo, then."

"Yes, thank you, good night. Sleep the first part of the night; you may be called."

I shut the door. C—— is already nodding in his chair. I rouse him, send him up to his buffalo. Sleepy as he is, he does not forget to say, "call me if there is a drum-roll. I want to have a hand at the threshing of those rascals if they pounce upon us in the night."

"Ah, Uncle Jeff, you won't say your prayers, I fear. You were cut out for a cruel soldier."

Uncle Jeff mounts up the wall-slats, saying, "I've written to my mother, that I can't say them, and she must keep saying them for me!" Little Daisy is slipping herself out of her shoes and stockings; saying, she is "so tired, so very tired; can she ever ride all the way to St. Louis? and will I make a calico bag for her cakes, so that they will not soil her carpet-bag? and how soon do I think Uncle Jeff's brother will be back to go home with her? If she could only get there before Christmas!"—"Before Christmas!" O, where will this persecuted people be before Christmas! Daisy does not know the creeping chill coming over me. She did not hear my question. She is fast asleep. Everybody is asleep. It is a long time since I undressed really. My dressing-gown bears me company nights, now, instead of days; because I like to be ready. Lucky that I am to-night. The door opens, and I open my eyes from my final nap. It is L——'s cheerful voice, asking me as he strikes a light, to help him off on a very dangerous express-ride, to present a letter to

Governor Shannon, at Westport. I am up in a moment. L—— looks sober, and as though the weight of years had rolled over him in one week. But he speaks up brightly, showing his fine teeth, which of themselves are a smile. I put him up a big paper of luncheon, for he is to pass into the heart of the enemy's country, who would see him die before they would give him a crumb of bread or a drop even of "cold water." He tells me of the council of war; how nobly all the wise and great men of the Territory had assembled; and how firmly they stood by each other. The first step to be taken, was, to address a letter of inquiries to Governor Shannon, to know why these tents of armed men were infesting our borders, committing depredations upon our people and harassing travellers who were going about their business; and requesting him to order their removal. The commander-in-chief appointed L—— to be the bearer of this despatch; and Babcock, the post-master, goes with him, probably with other despatches.

It is nearly twelve; a cloudy, lowering night, with gusts of chilly wind sweeping over the country. Our out-posts bring in word that our enemies are in a drunken row at Franklin. L—— must go past them. He knows their password; but it is a dangerous trip. Perhaps no better person could have been chosen. But he seems like my own boy, and my selfishness wishes they had chosen some one I did not know. I have this satisfaction, he will do himself honor wherever he goes and whatever is the result. I give him my *blessing;* while he says, quite in *short-hand,* " You will write to them all, if I do not return." I promise, and he passes out into the starless, moaning night.

Every one in the cabin has slept through it all; but my eyes are set open for the rest of the night. I hear the mounted guard ride round our cabin, with slow steps, as though they did not wish to wake the inmates. I listen as they advance out into the now dreary country. I hear distant fire-arms, and then more near. I know, now, that Missourians are just mean and cowardly enough to creep in upon us in the night; or to fire, as they have done, upon our watch, riding off as soon as they have done it. I wish Frank

Pierce had to stand on an open prairie and take his chance with better men. But that is not a good spirit to go to sleep on — so I dismiss it. I will close this, as there is a chance to send by express.

  Yours devotedly,   H. A. R.

MURDER OF BARBOUR.—THE TRUCE.

DECEMBER, 1855.

DEAR MOTHER OF MINE,—I yesterday closed a long package for you, sending it by private conveyance. But I should now feel as much lost without a letter begun to you, as I should be without knitting-work; and, as I invariably weave the stitches of a new stocking prospectively upon the needles from which one has just been completed, so I now turn to the table where are the papers, from which I have withdrawn all addressed to you, with the feeling that I must begin another stocking upon paper—gathering up the stitches of our cabin-life, and weaving them into a garment which I am quite sure will be warmly welcomed by you.

It is hardly twenty-four hours since L—— started on his perilous mission. But I cannot refrain from looking out occasionally for him. What absurd things we are always doing! He has gone fifty miles; has no chance of changing horse; not a very good road; several deep ravines to pass, difficult to cross; and a dark night to go over them. Two days certainly he must be absent, even if he escape the shots of the enemy; or, what is almost as much to be dreaded, being taken prisoner. Inside the cabin, everything remains as when I last wrote. Daisy gains strength slowly; walks like one upon stilts, tipping now this way, and now that. I have cut a pile of shirts for the boy; and, as I measure the dimensions, it dawns upon me, that he will not always be "the boy," for the size has much increased since the last were made.

Outside the cabin stands the pretty cow, Jennie, waiting for the ears of corn she knows very well she can coax from me when occasion calls me to the door. Meanwhile, she tugs slily at the bag, hoping to secure a morsel at once. Snuggled close by her is her six-months-old calf, for whom she seems to have more affection than other cows; or perhaps it may be because I never took so much notice of the relation between a cow and calf before. In this unfenced country, the only way to decoy a cow home, is, to tie the calf near the cabin. Our Jennie would have given up the hope of corn or pumpkin, sooner than the pleasure of coming to her baby. The haystack has still its party of hungry horses, diminishing its size at a frightfully rapid rate. And what is poor Jennie to do when winter sets in? I will not worry about any future. How can I, when I look over to the little town, blockading itself with forts and breastworks in every direction. How the men ply their shovels, working by turns of fifties, all day and all night! Around each fort, now the evening has come, are cords of blazing wood, to light them at their labor of defence; and over Fort Lane flutters a banner of stars and stripes, as an encouragement, as well as a protection. Alas, for the little town! How long could it stand against the power of a strong State, bearing down against it?

What a piece of news I have just heard! General Pomeroy taken prisoner, and in the camp below Franklin! He was here yesterday afternoon—said he was assailed at Westport, but frightened away his pursuers by pointing his pistol at them; and, when still nearer this place, forded the river three times to escape another band of ruffians. He seemed very tired, anxious, and uncertain for a time what course to pursue. He thought it very important for some one to go east for assistance. No one offered to go; and early in the afternoon he started off on this eastern enterprise, taking quite another route from that which passes the Missourian camps, and is usually travelled, as being the most direct to Kansas City. He crossed the Kansas river from the foot of Massachusetts street, landing in the Delaware country, intending to go down the course of the river on that side. But we have some Missourians living in this town who act as spies; and the General had gone but a short distance before he was captured. So much Typhoid has communicated; adding, that rumor said he was murdered. But I do not believe a word of that part. The idea of lynching a man so wide-awake and strong as he is, with his mild, clear eyes, his brown, good-humored face, reminding me always (I hope it won't look disrespectful to you, I'm quite sure it does not seem so to me) of the unreddened jams of the old, time-honored fire-places, such as were, in the time of wood, before coal was hoisted up into stoves for heating family rooms. No, I'm not going to believe but that I shall take him by the hand again in this world.

To-day has been as warm and pleasant as summer. The door stands open; cabin house-keeping has had a thorough overhauling; the broom has thrust itself into every chink and corner, most unceremoniously; pies are baking in the oven; and loaves of bread, just drawn from it, stand bottom up upon the board covering the flour-barrel. The "New York Journal of Commerce" performs the office of screening them from the dust-broom. Mr. ——, who has been away up the Territory, comes in upon me just as I have *not* finished; the litter being marshalled in the doorway, where he must step over it. I am so glad to see him! he has been so kind a friend. He comes to say, he is going home to Philadelphia at once. Does not look well, and fears sickness. He will return in the spring, with his wife. The tea-kettle sings upon the stove while we talk. I have smuggled the tea-pot, with fresh tea, and a portion of that noisy, singing tea-kettle, applied inwardly, alongside of it; coals are drawn out, the haunch of venison lifted down from the wall, slices broiled quickly, laid upon a hot plate, and placed before my pale, tired-looking friend, before he is aware of it. The tender meat and tea refresh him. We part at the door, he to go to his home, I to busy myself with the unsightly surface of things, underneath which home has made a grave, from which there can be no resurrection!

Well, here is the expected General, safe and sound, from the enemy's camp, and from the presence of Gov. Shannon! looking, indeed, as though he might have ridden fifty miles in six hours, and passed the intervening time of his absence without rest or sleep. But he was successful in his mission, the Governor promises to be here to-morrow.

And now comes another sorrowful item of intelligence. You know I wrote you about the faithful guardsmen who watch our little town while we sleep. Yesterday, one of them who lives upon a claim about six miles distant, mounted his horse, wholly unarmed, and started towards his home, which he had not visited for several days. Out over the wide prairie he sped his way, to gladden the hearts of his parents and dear wife; when he was met by some five or six Missourians, who commanded him to go with them. He answered that he was wholly unarmed, and on his route home to see his family; and putting spurs to his horse he kept on. Poor fellow! he little understood the cruel, heartless, dishonorable men with whom he had to deal. They aimed at the defenceless and wholly unconscious young man, and shot him in the back. He fell instantly from his horse. The released animal kept on his way, and trotted into the door-yard of the murdered man's friends. They, supposing he had got loose from his fastening in town, did not suffer at all from anxiety; but, fearing his gentle, timid wife, whose tears had hardly ceased to flow during the young soldier's absence, might put another construction upon this event, wisely kept it from her.*

---

* This statement I received from a lady with whom Mrs. Barbour remained a few days after her husband's murder. I have since learned, that two friends were near him when he was shot; that they did not know the ball reached him, until he had ridden some rods, when he uttered the cry, " My God! I am a murdered man!" and immediately slid from his horse to the ground; never spoke again, and breathed a few moments only.

Young Barbour's body was brought into town as soon as discovered, and laid away in one of the rooms of the new hotel, stretched out upon a seat, with his usual clothes upon him. He looked like one asleep; for the wound, though bleeding most profusely, did not disfigure him; it drew the color from his cheeks, that was all. His look of repose was even beautiful. He died, performing his duty.

The wife seemed wholly conscious that he was murdered, all the morning before the news was conveyed to his friends, though she lives six miles or more from here. How to bring her in with safety, was a matter of considerable importance, as enemies on horseback were supposed to be out in every direction. As the safest expedient, her husband's brothers, I think, dressed up in female apparel and accompanied her — women being allowed to pass without much question. It is quite impossible to describe the agony of this wife. She is a delicate, slight-built person, wholly devoted to this man; in fact, it seems to have been a perfect idolatry. Having no children, she centered her all of happiness upon him. The soldiers, who were witnesses to her distress, mingled their tears with her shrieks, while their blood stirred, naturally enough, for vengeance upon the murderers.

Gov. Shannon rides across the prairie with his suite and an escort sent out by Gen. Robinson. He occupies the back seat of a somewhat venerable-looking, two-horse buggy; and with the fine-looking horsemen in front and rear, makes a very respectable appearance. The upper chambers of the hotel are used as headquarters of our Kansas new-made officers. The windows are open; Gen. Robinson is preparing the somewhat restless body of soldiery, occupying the ground in front of the hotel, for the reception of Gov. Shannon. He points to the moving cavalcade in the distance, and says, it is in the hope of a speedy settlement, without more bloodshed, that this interview is proposed. It is not palatable to these men; for there is but a wall between them and their sleeping, murdered comrade. But they honor Gen. Robinson, and he curbs their justly indignant blood, by the power of his own magnanimity. The cavalcade passes through the opening crowd, to the hall of the hotel. Gen. Robinson comes down to the open door, to receive the Governor, and together they pass through the rudely-finished hall, by the murdered man, up the staircase, into a temporary council-chamber. In another chamber, a few rods distant, sits the new-made widow, weeping unconsciously; refusing food with such gentle violence as makes one feel as though they must gather her into their arms, and hush her to a sleep of total forgetfulness; for the multitude and noise without, added to her utter desolation within, have quite bewildered her.

Again the crowd open for the men of power to pass out. There is a call for cheers for Gov. Shannon. The cheering is more like a muffled drum, or the toll of bells, than a spontaneous outburst from a satisfied people.

Saturday is this eventful day. When will Saturday be the door-keeper of a Sabbath to us? Shall the Sabbath never immigrate? and the Commandments too?

The Sabbath-sun has set, and we have gathered round our cabin-fire, preparatory to a quiet evening of reading; when our good Doctor and his wife come in to see us. They are always welcome; but now they come, only to entice me out to the hotel, where people are to be introduced to the Governor, that he may judge for himself what kind of settlers Lawrence is honored with; and, for they have a double object, to make some arrangements for a peace party to be holden in that building on Monday evening. My first reply was in the negative. Public places are an aversion to me. The book, here by the tallow candle, on the quaint old table, is very much more to my taste. I offered to bake any amount of nicknacks for the party; but as for this introduction, what do I care for seeing a man for whom I can not reasonably entertain any respect.

No one could resist the quiet pleading of our Doctor's wife. So, in half an hour, we were all ushered into the council chamber of the third story. The room was quite filled with ladies. At the farther end stood Gov. Shannon. When he shook hands with me, he said, "What part of the country are you from?" I replied, somewhat proudly, "From that proscribed State, Massachusetts." He drew a chair for me, and seated himself by my side. He talked very well, rather too compromisingly. Occasionally he turned his head suddenly towards the window, reminding me (I suppose it was wicked) of that class of persons of whom it is written, they "flee when no man pursueth;" for it was evident he feared something. At last he gave expression to his thoughts and fears. A rumor had reached him that the people at the Missourian camp were so indignant towards him for coming up to Lawrence, that they would make an attack to-night, and lynch *him*, as well as destroy the town; he had, therefore, as a means of safety, sanctioned the commissions of Gen. Robinson and his staff, authorizing him to prepare for defence. I could not help replying, "You should have come to live among your own people, and then this trouble might never have come upon us," at the same time assuring him there was no man or woman here who would not feel bound in honor to protect him from every threatened danger. Indeed, I felt at the moment as though I could shoulder a rifle or point a pistol in his defence, if need be; not because of the man, but because he was the invited guest of Lawrence.

Gov. Shannon is a tall, well-built person, past fifty years of age, hair very gray and stiff, coarse features, pleasant eyes, and a benevolent crown to his forehead. But, to speak phrenologically, he has no firmness nor self-esteem; so that, when the baser portion of his nature does not rule over his more kindly and elevated powers, other people, no matter of what party or principle,—just whom he happens to be thrown in with,—sway him to their purposes. Like those gutta percha heads which the children used to have for playthings, twisting their features into every possible shape. Gov. Shannon has a set of features, purposes, and actions which are but the exponents of those who rule over him *pro tem.*

Nowithstanding the night passed off without alarm, the Governor did not choose to remain to the party. He gave sanction to our officers, and then turned his face towards the twelve hundred men who were encamped near Franklin, in order to command them to disperse. General Robinson and others accompanied him, having his promise that the prisoners, among whom was General Pomeroy, should be not only released, but placed beyond the reach of the mob. On their arrival,

General Robinson, with his usual magnanimity, addressed the people, endeavoring to show that much of this trouble had grown out of misunderstanding and misrepresentation; that the people on both sides, if they would but take the trouble to see and become acquainted with each other, would find a better state of things existing. He closed his remarks with an invitation for any who chose to take the trouble, to come to "the party,"—a party of peace and rejoicing that there was to be no more blood-shed.

Monday, 12 *o'clock at night.*—All the morning has been used up in various culinary preparations for the peace gathering. There are men here from every portion of the Territory; and the army is not to be disbanded till this offering of gratitude is over. L. came home for his supper rather earlier than usual, bringing with him two gentlemen, one the Mr. Jones who holds the office of sheriff under Gov. Shannon; the name of the other gentleman I do not remember. It has not been as often sounded in my ears as that of "Sheriff Jones." Both, however, were welcome to our cabin and to our stereotype supper of tea, corn-cake, and venison broiled upon the hot coals of black-walnut wood. As soon as serving was over, and my visitors were started off to the party, the "cook" took off her apron, slipped herself out of the warm folds of a woollen sack,—answering in a measure instead of plastered walls, to keep off the cold, —and, in less than half an hour, was introduced into the famous third-story council-chamber, now cheerfully lighted and agreeably warmed. Ladies and gentlemen had already begun to assemble; indeed, the whole building seemed alive with the hum of human voices. The illuminated windows sent forth a most unusual light across the night-shadows of the prairie. Sheriff Jones and his friend were in these upper rooms, being introduced to the ladies. They are both fine-looking men and of more than ordinary good breeding. Gen. Robinson, too, was showing them the attention they deserved at his hand, as invited guests. The General looked pale and more disturbed than I thought possible for one of such remarkable self-control and courage. It seemed that some of the hotel crowd were not ready to give up the war spirit, and accept with grace the peace-offering of social intercourse offered by our great-hearted General to those who had arrayed themselves so cruelly against us. And, although Sheriff Jones was nothing more nor less than an officer, acting under his oath of office, he became an apple of discord, because he was the only representative of Missouri. I have to confess to a feeling of mortification, that everybody could not at once bridge over the rapid current sweeping between these two contending parties, and let "by-gones be by-gones." But perhaps this feeling came to the surface because I had not entered into the atmosphere of bloodshed, and had not made the creation of awful "cartridges" the occupation of my leisure hours. Col. Lane's voice could be heard in different rooms, detailing to eager listeners the most painful circumstances of poor Barbour's death, and, with wonderful ingeniousness, keeping up the wicked spirit of vengeance among those over whom he exercised any power. What on earth he was driving at by such a course, it seemed to my stupid self quite impossible to understand; while, at the same time, I knew very well that he aimed at something he could not otherwise attain so well. Any reader of human faces can never study his without a sensation very much like that with which one stands at the edge of a slimy, sedgy, uncertain morass. If there is any good in him, I never, with all my industry in culling something pleasant from the most unpropitious characters, have been able to make the discovery. And he has not, in lieu of anything better, that agreeable fascination of manner which so often gives currency in society to men as hollow-hearted as he. Gen. Robinson stood like an aggrieved king. He not only stemmed the tide, but rolled back the surging emotions of the crowd; and the meeting closed much more like a gathering of peace than at one time seemed likely. I should like very much to have you see Gen. Robinson. He is honest in expression, simple and unaffected in manner, and brave as a lion. I have somewhere seen a fine engraving of John Knox, standing with uplifted finger and solemn, earnest rebuke in his countenance, in the presence of Queen Mary. The head, profile, and general outline of figure are very much that of Gen. Robinson.

I believe I have forgotten to tell you that the funeral of Mr. Barbour was deferred, on account of the important business this week to be attended to. Another week has closed, and the Sabbath calls all people out to pay the last tribute of respect to poor Barbour's memory. A December day, but clear, cloudless, dreadfully bright, and windy. The mud is deep as one's boots; goes up over rubbers without any apparent doubts as to the propriety of such an innovation. Yet, the whole, neighborhood seems astir with people, picking their way to one centre — the *hotel*, where not as last Monday evening, for rejoicing, they come together; but to mourn with the sufferers of a great sorrow: a widow, made so by violence wholly unprovoked; brothers, bereaved in a manner never to be forgotten — never to be thought of in years to come but with the smartest twinges of pain. The room we enter is a long dining-hall. The walls are of limestone, rough and unplastered. Seats of plank stretch in rows, closely packed, through the whole length, with the exception of a narrow space for the clergyman. The seats are all filled. The atmosphere of the assembly is of the truest sympathy. Each soul seems personally aggrieved and afflicted. Silence is the only, and most emphatic, expression given to this grief. The first break upon that silence is the tread of many feet and a smothered, broken sob, that will not be wholly choked down. Working his way through the crowd, appears a tall man, with white hair, large blue eyes, and a very benevolent countenance. You see at once that he is a Methodist. He has clinging to his arm a small, veiled figure, — everybody knows 'tis the widow; "a widow indeed."

There comes another smothered sob as she is borne along to the far end of the hall. The man of white hair stoops over her tenderly and whispers words of peace to her. I do not hear them; she does not. Now she sinks into a seat. A hymn is read, and the crowd sing the tune of "Martin Luther," so familiar to everybody, and stretching back over the whole length of oldest life present. What a relief it is! how it gathers up and rolls away the pent-up emotions of the multitude!

Now the white-head sinks down over bended knees, to the floor, and his voice utters its prayers and supplications, while the tears course down the cheeks of the speaker and his audience. The sobs of that broken heart grow fainter. Does she find a relief through the channel of other hearts? I believe so. Then follow short speeches from Col. Lane and Gen. Robinson, and a sad sermon from the white-head. All the exercises are remarkably good of the kind. Even Col. Lane did well.

The services are over, and the people form a procession. Men with arms reversed take the lead; then the body and its friends; then the whole crowd, mounted in carts drawn by oxen, wagons led by mules, and carriages of every pattern, form into a solemn line stretching far along the open country. Up over Mount Pleasant curves the road to the ground appropriated for a burial place, two miles away. What a sight it is! One like it could hardly be got up anywhere else, or under any other circumstances. This grand old country, venerable with its lofty trees, its smoothly terraced hills, its serene repose,—where the moccasin only has trod as at home, and crept away in by-places to take the sleep of death! The tread of the white man is fresh and new; but to-day the grand old prairie witnesses the burial of its second martyr! Now the soldiers make a wall on either side, with lifted hats, for the mourners to pass through. Gently the coffin is lowered to its last rest, while the words, "Dust to dust," "I am the Resurrection and the Life," are broken by the wailing wind, and lost to the ears of the audience by the fast-coming sobs of that forlorn, childless, earth-stricken widow! The soldiers now approach; the audience and friends fall back, giving place to them; while, standing about the grave, at the signal of their commander, "Uncle Jeff," one division after another bury the contents of their rifles in the last resting-place of their much-loved and honored comrade.

Wednesday. — The people from different portions of the Territory have departed from Lawrence, and we fall back again into the usual routine of a new settlement. In the early part of the month almost everybody was busy, trying to make their places of abode more suitable for the coming winter. When destruction threatened the town, of course all personal thrift and comfort were lost sight of in the general danger. Now winter seems to hurry in upon us with unusual severity; and so great has been the tax upon the strength of us all for the last three weeks of sleepless anxiety, that all effort, just now, seems quite impossible.

I cannot rid myself of the impression, that more danger lies ahead. I do not forget the long distance stretching between us and our friends; the frozen rivers, cutting off the usual means of intercourse; and the falling snow, making our way trackless in any direction. North, south, or west, there can be seen no help for us in an emergency. Our eyes overleap all points but the *East*; and, alas! between us and *our* East, there looms up a fearful Ogre, in the shape of the State of Missouri! Perhaps a class of immigrants of so high an order in cultivation, natural ability, or energetic foresight and calculation, never before planted themselves as the nucleus of a new State, as are these exiles from home in Kansas. Ultraism, naturally or by education, is not the order of mind prevailing among them. Old and early habits of conservative obedience to the "powers that be"—the laws under which they grew up and found both liberty and protection—still cling to them; and it would be strange if the experience of the past few weeks did not make these habits more clear and honored than ever before.

The man who by his acts destroys our faith in him, robs us of an inheritance wider than the circumference of any one man, be he ever so great, because he undermines the foundation of our trust in others.

How we, at the North, have always believed implicitly in the chivalry of the South, and the wide-hearted generosity of the West. It is not till we arrive in Kansas, away from everything dear and familiar, away from all the ordinary comforts of older countries, that the truth really dawns upon us. Mother, there is no indignity to be mentioned which has not been heaped upon us. By it I feel myself robbed of a large estate—my faith in human nature. I cannot understand at all the ground of our offence. If we are poor, should not that be a reason why our neighbors' sympathy and cordial aid should be poured in upon us? Why don't they call and see these poor, benighted "Yankees;" and out of their abundance, give us help? Surely this vast region furnishes room for all! Missouri is larger than New England, and sparsely populated. I am not wise enough to understand why, but it seems as though *land* had been a bone of contention ever since the earth was created. Just now it is all a "muddle" to me; and as I do not know how to moralize, or you care to hear me, I will subscribe myself,

Your most affectionate daughter,

H. A. R.

WINTER EXPERIENCES AND OBSERVATIONS.

FEBRUARY, 1856.

MY DEAR MOTHER, — You will feel anxious, to have a whole month pass by without even a word from us. It has, however, been the fault of no one. Soon after closing my last, sickness and the most freezing cold weather entered hand-in-hand into the cabin. Both were wholly unexpected guests, and quite unprepared for. The cold never took such a fearful grasp of this country before, within the memory of Indian or missionary. The cabins of new settlers, from necessity poor at best, are made with the understanding that winters here are not severe. Think of the thickness of a "shake" only, between one and the cold measuring twenty degrees below zero!

A sorry sort of experience the past month has been to our little household; cheered very often, it is true, by the great kindness and constant attention of people about us;

yet, dreary in its details. A bed of "prairie feathers" is not very comfortable at any time; and warmth is not one of its inherent qualities, under any circumstances. Every twenty-four hours, almost, brought some accession to the snow-drifts, and filled the atmosphere of cabins with a most subtle, throat-cutting element, almost impossible to breathe. Large cooking stoves, well heated, made but little headway in a contest so unequal. The wood was not always dry; and to keep it in a decent state for the fire, it was piled up in the cabin, out of the full force of the oft-recurring snow storms. Late in the autumn, L—— had gone up into the territory on important business, and been obliged to camp out without the usual preparation travellers make when it is their intention to sleep under the stars. He and his companion lost their way. They had but two matches left, and expended a good deal of unavailing effort before they succeeded in finding anything dry enough to kindle a fire with. The wind took possession of the first match as soon as it ignited. You can better imagine than I describe the state of two wanderers, totally at a loss how to "define their position," in the darkness of a November night, many miles from any habitation, on a prairie unmarked by any lines of travelled roads, and a storm lowering over their heads! One match left! With the greatest care, not unmingled with proportional fear as to results, it was lighted. Some good angel must have spread its wings of safe protection between the tiny flame, and the winds which monopolize every point of compass, for the fire was lighted. Heaps of wood were piled up, the wagon drawn near enough to shelter the heads of the two young men; the horses sheltered by the "timber," corn given them, and a portion roasted in the fire for the supper of our travellers. With their feet towards the fire and heads under the wagon, they went to sleep, and did not wake till the fire was out by the intrusion of rain and snow, and their persons were crusted over entirely by the frozen mixture. Daylight was worth more than anything else, and that was now about them. With the hope and elasticity belonging not only to the young, but almost inherent in the wild freedom of western life, the horses were harnessed and a point taken, to reach if possible some place of shelter and refreshment. At ten o'clock a cabin appeared under the shelter of a wild and most picturesque bluff; and our guests were most cordially welcomed by its only inhabitant, a German immigrant.

L—— has often told me, since, that he never experienced so great a surprise. The *welcome* he expected, because there are no more hospitable people than the far-off, wide-apart "squatters" on Uncle Sam's farm. This German, however, fed them with venison, rubbed down the almost perishing horses, and then gave his guests an intellectual treat of the rarest kind. His mind seemed full of the finest specimens of culture, and his enthusiasm over Nature's wild beauty in this western world, seemed almost boundless. L—— and his companion felt quite ill-used and frozen, through the evening; but the compensation of the morning, and indeed the whole day and night, through which they remained as guests to the kind German, was more than an equivalent for all they suffered.

When the cold days of Christmas pressed down upon us, we felt as though we were to go through another edition of L.'s experience on the prairie. Our spirits held out very remarkably. Things did not look any worse than they really were—which, to be sure, were bad enough. Sickness pressed heavily upon me; but the fever made me quite insensible to the danger from the cold air, until, like poor "Joe," I began to heave hard for my breath, like one laboring with an oar. Now that it is past, there come to my mind distinct pictures, vivid, and most touching, of that period. A group of three, snuggled close round the stove, vainly endeavoring to get warm, leaving it in haste to get more wood, to place a hot brick about my person, or to break the ice for me to drink. For some time I refused to have any watcher, it seemed too cold for any one to stay out of bed. Alice was placed under cover very early in the evening. Water was all I craved, and it would freeze solid before midnight. Edward tried the experiment of boiling some, filling a mug with it, and placing the mug in a tin pail, covered tight. This answered very well awhile; but at last the mug froze down in the pail, so that it could not be got out without being set on the stove. At this time E. seemed quite tired out with care and anxiety. One night he went to bed early, leaving a great fire. It was about nine when I took up my tumbler to drink — it was frozen solid. In a moment the door opened for Mr. W.; my sight was very dim and he looked a long way off, and the bed seemed to have been moved back into another room. I tried to speak; but could not make a sound. I beckoned to him; for I did not realize that the fault was mine that he seemed so far away. He saw my movement, came to give me the tumbler, saw that it was full of ice, and went to the pail, which was in the same condition. He replenished the fire, took up the pail and vanished. The air was full of a driving snow-storm; and it was a long way to the spring; but very soon the pail and man returned into the cabin. I had not only a "cup of cold water," but a dish of nice cocoa, brought as soon as it could be made. L. came in, in a few moments, and remained the rest of the night. He says it was the only time in his life when he thought he was in danger of freezing; and that, with the largest fire he could build, the water for me to drink froze upon the stove-hearth!

Towards night the next day, I was roused from a stupid sleep by the entrance, first, of a fair and delicate-looking woman, then the Dr., L., Mr. W., and several others. The lady announced to me that I was to be moved immediately, and proceeded at once to tuck the clothes closely about the narrow bed, and to spread a woollen shawl over my head; the gentlemen then raised me up, bed and all, bore me out the door, and placed me in a cart as gently as a mother could have laid away a babe. The company mounted in about me, holding a buffalo-skin over the bed. The ride was not at all painful to me, and I did not feel the cold in the least.

The famous hotel, which has quite a history of its own, notwithstanding its youth, was soon reached. It stands up quite high from the ground; had no steps yet made; and to enter, an inclined plane of boards rested upon the sill and the ground. The stairs, too, in the hall, as yet existed only in the mind of the master-builder. The space they were to occupy was covered with narrow strips of board; and as one flight rose over the other, from the cellar up four stories, it was enough to make any head dizzy to take themselves up, without the weight of a bed and sick person.

Now that I am well, I cannot but consider it a remarkable feat that all these uncertain steps were taken without injury to any one. My head was not uncovered till the door of L.'s office had shut me in, and the bed settled down by the side of a wall, covered with law books, the odor from which awakened most pleasant remembrances of home. Those who have had the sensation of a heavy plank bound over the lungs, can understand how great the relief was to breathe the warm air of this comparatively warm and finished room. It was a long and narrow place, with one window looking to the south; walls on two sides, of cemented lime-stone, very rough, with occasional chinks through which the sky was visible. The other sides were thin partitions, dividing it on one side from the "council-chamber," and on the other from the powder-magazine! Still farther along the hall, Mr. W. had secured a room for himself. At night a mattress was drawn by my bed-side, and there L. and E., alternately tending the fire and nursing me, passed the time till morning.

On the other side, close to me, was drawn another lounge, where, in the unbroken sleep of childhood, little Alice securely rested. About this room there has always seemed the atmosphere of the utmost peace and security; and hereafter, in years to come, these young people will, I think, forget all that it was at the time so hard to bear, and remember it as one of the periods of safe-keeping, and active mental growth.

Meanwhile the snow and cold seem to keep time with each other. The hum of voices in the council chamber is increased by numbers. Matters of importance are before its members. We are startled often by the report of fire-arms.

There is a stone building nearly opposite, in one part of which is a tailor's shop. Living somewhere in this settlement is a creature, half man, half brute, who sometimes allows the one nature to rule him, and sometimes the other—a noisy, uproarious bully, when warmed up with whiskey, called "Buckskin." Some real or imaginary cause of offence has sprung up between him and this tailor, opposite. The brute-nature has rule over Buckskin to-night;

his grievance, whatever it may be, is athirst for vengeance. Loud and awfully profane talking peals forth from his mouth at this puny strip of a tailor, who shuts and bolts his door for safety, putting out the light within. Buckskin fires through the door and window, shot after shot. We are in great anxiety, expecting to hear of the tailor's murder. Quite a mob have collected in the street. What a strange sight this would be in Boston! and how quickly the strong hand of a Boston policeman would lead away the aggressor, and disperse the gathering multitude! Late into the night the sounds die out; even Buckskin must have sleep.

Sheriff Jones has had quite a novel finale to an arrest. The wife of the arrested man should have been born on the other side of the Atlantic; and would have made a fitting mate to some modern Robin Hood. In the first place, she hid the Sheriff's dragoon coat, which in itself was very valuable as well as a necessary appendage this cold weather. After her husband was placed in the carriage for removal, she drew a loaded pistol from her person, pointed it at Sheriff Jones, and declared she would fire if he did not release her husband. As there seemed no possible doubt of her sincerity, and as the gentleman could not avenge himself upon a woman, he released the man — expressing the opinion, that he should rather face an army of men than one furious woman. More recently, that same woman went into a yard of horses kept to let, and demanded one, over which she had some real or imaginary right, presenting at the same time her pistol at the hostler. The shock to his sensibility was so great, that he suffered her to mount the horse and ride off without molestation. This reminds me of another "strong-minded woman." When at the peace party, the Doctor called my attention to a woman, sitting very straight in a chair, quite near an illuminated window, by the light of which she was reading a newspaper. Her eyes were very black; her face not only determined, but somewhat brazen. The Doctor amused himself, as well as me, by detailing some of her freaks during our troubles. In one instance, when her cabin was visited by the enemies, she passed herself off as a Missourian, and, through the statement of her defenceless position, gained from them two rifles! On another occasion, when going home from Lawrence, the distance from which is about six miles, she rode her own horse and led that of her husband, who, being one of the soldiers, could not return with her. After riding about half way home, she saw a man hastening after her; and, when within speaking distance, he demanded the extra horse. She replied, "Take it if you can," and put her pony into a fast trot. Stimulated both by the ride and her nearer approach to her home, she, when at a good distance, reined in her horse and laughed at him for not taking what he wished. The pursuer got very angry; he was drunk before; he drew his pistol but had not steadiness of nerve to hold it, and it slipped from him to the ground. Fearing, half drunk as he was, to dismount, he started on to secure the horse, uttering oath after oath. My lady's spirit was now up, she did not fear a drunken man on horseback, so she made a wide circuit, bringing herself back to where the pistol lay; it was but the work of a moment for her to jump to the ground, secure the prize, spring upon the horse, and gallop home.

The quiet of the hotel, hitherto broken only by the click of the workmen's hammers, or the hurried step of its few inmates, has suddenly changed. There are armed men quartered again in the rooms directly beneath us. Steps of many people press along the entries to the "council-chamber." Soberness settles over the faces which have borne so lightly and bravely the vexatious inconveniences of a first winter in a new country. Dame Rumor has issued her bulletin, that our little town is to be burned, and women and children must be removed or share the massacre of men.

The forts have miserable shanties erected in them for the soldiers stationed in each. The cold increases. Officers sleep upon the floor of the council-chamber. Over our heads, upon the flat roof of the hotel, we hear the steady, measured tread of a sentinel. The sound is crisp and cold, with the deep snow still increasing, driven furiously by the wind. Each soldier at the different quarters takes his hour's tramping watch. There is over all a fearful sense of forsaken helplessness. It seems almost as though heaven and earth had forsaken us. Our officers, however, are strong and brave men; they stand like a wall of fire between us and danger. But how few of them in numbers! Who among you whom we left at home can ever reckon up the wear and tear that these men are passing through? The half-sleeping posture upon the floor or a rude bench; the family, left at home without its rightful protection; and the constant, reliable impression that attack is inevitable, and that no sufficient force is ready to meet it.

Almost every day brings some few fresh hands and true hearts into the town. Very often our door is opened by mistake, and men rush close to the fire, regardless of everything but to warm themselves. I amuse myself scrutinizing their various wrappings, — an odd mixture of Indian gay blankets, leggins, and moccasins, with the remnants of a former civilization in the shape of gloves, caps, and coats. Stupid people, we have none. The hard attrition of border life, and the granite roughness of every circumstance surrounding us, brings to the surface every available element of human capability. I can readily imagine how, unsanctified with a righteous cause, this surface-power may become cruel and vindictive.

Now, to the tramp of the watchmen overhead is added the more distant tread of a wide-awake sentinel in the long hall, upon the first floor. Early in the morning the soldiers are astir. Their cook regales us by the pleasant flavor of his coffee and broiled beef, to say nothing of corn-mush and hot biscuit. Like all invalids, for want of other employment, I trace his march through breakfast, the orders for more water, for towels to wipe the dishes with, intermingled with the clatter of cups and saucers, snatches of pleasant songs, uproarious laughter, and jokes quite unintelligible to us up above; though we cannot resist the magnetic influence to join the laugh. Then there is a sudden rush at the material for dinner. No joke, this, in a freezing day — to cook for a company of soldiers, and the days so short. Sometimes the meat burns with the hurry, or the mush binds itself to the bottom of the kettle, or the water boils out from the potatoes. Every housekeeper knows how very unpleasant the odor ascending from such a culinary failure is.

This settled routine is at length broken in upon, at *midnight*, by the arrival of a courier from Fort Leavenworth. The council are awakened to hear the news of another murder at Easton, where an election was held; and a request for assistance in the shape of armed men.

There is no more sleep in the hotel. Men are selected to start out immediately as far as the house of Sicoxie, a friendly Delaware Indian, and there remain for their orders from Leavenworth. Three men are to keep on, one of whom is L——, to get accurate information about the murder.

To-day, Captain Dicky, of Topeka, follows their march, with quite a company. The distance is about thirty miles, I believe, through an unbroken road, a wild Indian country. Captain Brown lived but a few hours after his wounds were inflicted. He was taken prisoner by men from Platte county, and confined in a room, to be hung the next morning; but, so greedy were his captors for his blood, that, before he was really led out of the entrance to his prison, hatchets were raised above his head and bowie-knives thrust into his body.

He fell most barbarously wounded. At his earnest request, he was placed in a wagon and taken to his home, where, on his arrival, he had time enough to bid farewell to his wife and children.

Capt. Brown was born at the South; emigrated from Ohio to this Territory with his family, and located near Fort Leavenworth. In the autumn he came to Lawrence, and remained till our safety was no longer in jeopardy. In personal appearance he was quite a marked man, even in a crowd. He was unusually tall, with a rich, brown complexion, dark, abundant hair and beard, and eyes large, dark, and sad in expression. I do not think that any one who ever saw him will forget his personal appearance, and no dweller in Kansas can ever forget the mark his cruel death has made upon the pages of its early history.

Capt. Dicky arrived on Saturday evening. They came across the river at the foot of Massachusetts street, and rode up in front of this hotel, where they were received with loud cheers. Certain military manœuvres, quite unintelligible to my ignorant self, were performed, interspersed with cheers, speeches, and other testimonials of rejoicing. It really was a grand display. The moonlight, glittering upon the snow; the fantastic, distorted shadows of curious cabins, piles of lumber, wood, and sleds of an entirely new pattern, stretching out on every side; the immense, rude, unfinished hotel, looming up behind the smoking, tired horses, mounted with men quite as originally dressed and as truly brave as were the men of old revolutionary times! After going through the (I suppose usual) courtesies of military tactics on similar occasions, the company galloped, in single file, to temporary places of shelter for their tired horses; and soon after refreshed themselves with a supper, prepared for them at a restaurant close by; then accepted the hospitality of the hotel, wherein people are stowed away for a night's rest, very much as trunks and boxes are packed into a warehouse.

The distinctive lines between those who live for themselves and those who live for others, are never so clearly defined as in a new, yet unpossessed country. I cannot give you a faithful transcript of our own daily experience, without telling something of the kind acts of strangers, who prepare for us nice delicacies in the shape of broiled birds, prairie chickens, and rabbits, accompanied with wheat-bread and ginger-cakes. Our box in the corner, bearing upon its top our small pattern of china and delf, rarely fails to sustain some nice little mess, carefully covered with a napkin or newspaper to secure it alike from the gaze of visitors, the dust of a dirty room, and the cunning mice, who between four and five o'clock descend from the upper portion of the cemented walls, creeping out from the smallest little crevices, and travelling at the most rapid rate, to the floor below. The little curious creatures have, as a race, most inquiring minds. There is no space of this room which they have not measured with their rapid feet; and no secret hiding-place they have not peered into. Harmless always, except in taking a bite of everything eatable, they make themselves perfectly at home. If the room is still, they amuse me by their frolics upon the floor; and often they play "'possum," by rolling themselves up and dropping from the stone wall down to the floor below.

Often, in the night, they make a short cut across the bed's head, springing thence to the books, scrambling among the papers, for a night's entertainment. Woe be to any delicacy, if they get at it! We learn at home to say, "still as mice," but that saying grew out of ignorance of this miniature race of creatures. One should be deaf, to sleep well where they are. Such dissipated night merry-makings as they have can hardly be recorded of any other race; and their grace of motion is beautiful indeed.

There are a large proportion of remarkably pretty women in Lawrence. Most of them married, yet quite young; indeed, I consider myself, for the first time in my life, quite venerable when compared with those about me. Living in a "shake" cabin, close under my window, is the fair little lady who helped me into my present "quarters." She is from Ohio. Her place of abode, with its one window towards me, its chimney of stove pipe, its tiny tallow candle of an evening, is always an object of interest; a cold little home it is. Her feet have frozen this cold winter while busy about her house-work. There was a gathering moisture in her eye when she told me; but the quiver about the mouth passed into her usual smile of cheerful hopefulness, and absorbed the tears before they fell. With more than usual interest I have watched her one room, the past week. She has taken in a sick man, Major Robinson, of Tecumseh, who for some time has been rather sick, at the "Cincinnati House." That is no place for sick people. This man has fallen into good hands; but he is quite unconscious of those about him. Sweet forgetfulness spreads a mantle over his present, and memory takes him back to other days, and to his early home. He holds long talks with his mother. Almost his last request is, "Mother, take off my shoes; my feet are tired and swollen, I cannot travel any farther to-night." And so, in a state of pleasant surroundings, a happy unconsciousness of his present condition, he passes into the other life, where every want may be met, without opposition. I know when his life ceases; for the lady brings out the bed-clothes and stretches them upon the line. My friend from Paschal Fish's, formerly of Roxbury, with another beautiful woman from Worcester, step out with saddened faces, and walk quickly away. Poor fellow! he had no relative near him at the close of his life, but there are good, kind people everywhere; and under their blessed ministry he passed away. The body, once placed in its coffin, is brought to this depot of all things, whether living or dead. This shelter is the last resort; the place, too, for all assemblies, whether of business, pleasure, meetings for prayers, or, as in this instance, services for the dead. Many days passed before the honors due to this brave young officer were attended to. The accumulating snow and freezing cold were a very tolerable excuse, yet not enough to satisfy those who had consciences. At last people assembled in respectable numbers; company A. trod the white, almost unbroken snow, as escort, far out of town to the appropriate burial-ground.

E. goes up the river in company with several men every day, to haul down wood upon the ice. They wrap up as warm as though we had suddenly exchanged climates with Labrador. People are very busy cutting ice from the river; and, although our ears are not enlivened with the merry jingle of bells, we are very much amused at the numberless new inventions in the shape of sleds and sleighs that are each day coming into town. The business portion of Lawrence has always more or less of the Indian tribes within its capacious street. Delawares and Shawnees mingle among our people very pleasantly, and are not much to be distinguished from them in dress this winter,—for our men resort to buffalo or blanket, as the most comfortable promenade dress. Other tribes of Indians, living farther west and less civilized, leading rather wandering lives, pitch their tents in the "timber bottom-lands" not far distant, and come hither for their food. I have amused myself not a little, sitting by this window, so high above the ground and overlooking every building in sight, watching the movements of these Indians. This afternoon is as cold as possible, the snow dry and frozen stiff; some wild-looking specimens have come up the street, fastening their ponies to a pile of wood near a grocery store. One of the squaws has set down a tall red bag close beside the walls of a cabin; presently she brings two bags of flour round near her pony. She proceeds to take off the saddle, produces a leather strap from her pocket, ties a bag of flour to each end of the strap, and balances them by means of the strap thrown over pony's back. Now the saddle is replaced and girted tightly on. Pony is very patient, being evidently well acquainted with his mistress' movements. There are some small packages, too, which she fits on some safe way, at least I hope so, for my attention is suddenly arrested by the shrill cry of a baby, and my eyes astonished by the appearance of a pair of little hands and arms thrust out through the red flannel bag. The mother expedites her packing business, springs quickly up over the flour on to the saddle, while a tall Indian suddenly turns the corner, lifts red flannel and its wondrous contents into her lap, over which she spreads a blanket, smothering any further attempts at crying which the ill-used infant might have had in view. Another woman, mounted in the same way, appears in the street. Both ponies so heavily laden pass slowly down to the river and cross to the Delaware country, which stretches along the opposite bank of the Kansas river, and is densely wooded.

It is not till the middle of Februrary that the winter relents—the eaves of our humble dwelling begin to drip; and travelling up and down the river with loaded teams is set aside as unsafe. The winter has indeed been a long and trying one. Provisions have become scarce, and the difficulty of providing for so many men, a question of the utmost interest to wise men. Everybody has denied themselves luxuries most cheerfully. But the goal of a fruitful summer, the nearer relief even of access to our friends, through the opening navigation of the western rivers, all seem a long way off. The unbridged streams between this place and the nearest market-town in Missouri, together with the now softening drifts of snow, make all market communication quite impossible. All through the winter our mails have been most unfaithfully attended to; to speak fairly, one half of our letters and papers never get through the two borders of our most truly interesting neighbor, Missouri. Numerous money-drafts, forwarded from the East to help us in our utmost need, have been detained. I should certainly be obliged, in face of all I have seen and learned this winter to accept the awful doctrine of total depravity, if it were not for my firm conviction that there is a great misunderstanding somewhere. Certainly there must be a great proportion of good and kind people in the State of Missouri; this, however, is simply a matter of *faith*, not of *sight*. To us, however good they may be, they turn a deaf ear and keep a cold silence.

Feb. 22*d.* — This twenty-second of February witnesses a social gathering in the hall of this hotel, or rather in the dining-room. "Company A" give the party, and preside over it with a great deal of hospitality. Tables are spread in the upper entry, which is very spacious. I am quite surprised at the clean and nice appearance of the tables, and the variety spread upon them for our refreshment. In the course of the evening, "Company A" entertain us with an original song got up by them, in the ballad style, giving quite a history of this settlement. This company is a matter of general interest to us all. Its members are young men, and very brave. One of its members, a native of Ohio, has in several instances shown remarkable presence of mind. Very early in the commencement of this settlement a tented cabin took fire, there was no person in it, but there were some trunks of clothes belonging to absent members of the settlement, and also, a *keg of powder*. Persons who saw the fire knew the cabin could not be saved. With a sudden cry at the remembrance of the powder, young B. sprang down the slope, entered the burning curtain, and took the cask, already smutty and slightly charred, in his arms, and running out still farther down the ravine, threw it from him, and then returned and hauled out the trunks in safety. Another young man, from New England, succeeded in getting a team, loaded with cannon, up from Kansas City, when camps on the road were filled with armed men.

Feb. 24*th.*—The ice in our river dissolves its winter-union to-day—this twenty-fourth day of February—a bright, cheerful Sabbath. The sky appears in its own peculiar clearness, bringing distant objects distinctly before the eyes. I go from one window of the hotel to another, uttering exclamations at the prospect. I see the river curving quite round, up towards its source, walled with tall, tastefully arranged trees, and, floating sluggishly upon its surface, cakes of ice thick enough to have done justice to a more northern latitude. Groups of people stand along the shore, watching with apparent interest the indications of a clear and navigable river. While, from many little homes, church-going people pick their way through the softened snow, pools of dirty water, and mud of uncertain depth, towards the rude place of worship. Off in the distance, towards the south-west, Blue Mound lifts its fair proportions against the sky, making a line with the Wakarusa river, marking its course by the fringe of trees along its nearest banks; and its farther shore, by the rising, terraced slopes lifting themselves far in the distance to the line of the horizon, sprinkled here and there with patches of clean snow, upon a ground of dried grass and the black mould of this truly fertile country. Without any great stretch of the imagination, one can fancy many distant towns and villages nestled in those pleasant slopes. One can never look over this beautiful country without a feeling of astonishment that it was never taken up for settlement before.

The month of February closes full of hope and cheerfulness to us all. The winter is indeed gone, and our places of abode are still standing unmolested. The hour of my imprisonment, too, is nearly out. We must go back to cabin house-keeping soon; and till then, believe me as ever, your affectionate daughter, H. A. R.

KANSAS SUFFERERS. — TROUBLE THREATENED.

MARCH, 1856.

MY DEAR MOTHER, — Your most kind and acceptable letter reached me in the same mail with Sarah's, and gave me so great a start, lest something unpleasant had occurred, that I hardly dared break the seals. Since receiving them I have written to Ellen, so that you will, if it reaches you, know how much better I am. We moved back to the cabin last Monday. It was hardly warm enough weather to make the change, but the men were plastering the hotel, and I felt as though they would be glad to have us leave. Besides, I recollected the theory you always advanced, that plastering, when fresh, was a dangerous near-neighbor. The two first nights after I came into the cabin I coughed almost incessantly. The fire went out, and the rough winds crept in everywhere. But it seemed pleasant to get back once more and brighten up the cabin with a warm fire, and a general washing of dishes, and dusting of furniture.

We have made another improvement, too, by covering two-thirds of the floor with carpeting. On that portion we have the bed, bureau, washstand, grandpa's chair and the little table. The carpet reaches close to one side of the cooking-stove; and in front of the stove I have a thick mat, upon which my feet now rest as I write. The children have just gone down to the bank of the river, to see a skiff launched.

Kansas river is now a deep and rather good-looking stream, but lacks motion and a clear bottom. The ice is out as far as St. Louis, but no boats have come up yet; and travelling any other way is too hard for people. So far, I have seen no improvement upon our New England climate. One can but consider themselves most seriously taken in, by all the grand talk about Kansas winters. The Delawares, however, say this is the coldest winter for very many years. Indeed, they warned us last fall, by various signs, to prepare for a cold winter. But how could we get ready to be comfortable, while watching the signs so much more momentous—of war! And how could people make tight houses, without lumber? Sawmills and grist-mills should have preceded printing-presses in the proportion of a dozen to one. Then, the little money among us would have gone much farther. Many a field of corn was lost because the owner was on guard in Lawrence, when he should have been gathering his crops; and many a bag of meal was emptied, and many a quarter of beef was roasted, gladly and generously, to feed the soldiers. These things, in a country so new, have of course left their effects upon the whole winter. There has been a great scarcity of money, and of many things which money alone could buy. It is not possible for those who sit in whole houses and by warm fires, to understand this winter, out in Kansas. Those who have been on the spot and passed through its own peculiar history, must always consider it as a rich legacy in the line of experience.

I really wish I had more births and marriages to report to you, with fewer deaths. The former, I am sorry to say, are quite unusual in the present epoch of Kansas history. In this respect our history is quite in character with the history of the early settlement of other States and Territories; the graveyard is one of the first apportionments, and the soonest to be thickly inhabited. Quite late in the autumn, one of our merchants returned east to bring his wife out here. She died of cholera on the Missouri river, and was buried where many other immigrants have found a last resting-place, upon its wild, uninhabited banks. The forlorn husband, Mr. Wilder, continued his journey, and reached this place in safety. He inherited consumptive tendencies, and this sad misfortune aggravated and increased them. He died this week. He had made every preparation to return to his former home in Vermont, and waited only for better weather and better travelling. They both came too late.

My first escape from the winter prison was at the invitation of Typhoid, to pass the day with her. It is of necessity a crowded, depot-like house; people always coming to warm themselves and departing, or getting a night's lodging and then going on their way bright and early in the morning.

On this gala-day for me, there was still

some snow and frost about the earth, and a curious — between "*hay* and *grass*" — aspect of people, cattle, and equipages. Carts, with oxen or horses attached, stood side by side with sleds of most *extemporaneous* build; while men with blankets or coats, or without either, carefully picked their busy way to and from the town. At noon, strangers and boarders accept the call of the house-bell, and flock in for dinner. While in the midst of the gathering aspirants for dinner, a yoke of red and white oxen drag a most rare pattern of a sled close before the door-steps. The man guiding the oxen is very young; and he seems remarkably careful of his load. How could he be otherwise? for she is a beautiful young girl, dressed in refined taste, notwithstanding the rude sled and the clumsy bed-comforter with which she is so carefully wrapped. She takes a seat by the sitting-room fire; is very cold, and prefers the warmth to dinner. On our return from the dining-room, she is absorbed in the perusal of letters just brought her by her husband from the post-office. She is so pretty, and so young-looking, one cannot refrain from gazing at her, and wondering how she came out here. Without undue curiosity, the impalpable atmosphere about persons gives you some kind of a clue to their condition.

This lady finished her letters, read them over a second time, then wrapped them up carefully and placed them in her basket. She was too young and unsuspicious not to trust those about her. She seemed to crave sympathy; and began the story one most wished to hear. She lived on a claim out ten miles, on the road up the river, a very lonesome place. If they only could live in the town. She always had lived in a town before. But now she had spoken to but two women out of the house since September; and there was no travelling past, wherewith to amuse herself. To be sure, her husband's mother lived with them, and was very kind; what would they do without her? And the house was more comfortable than any she passed in her ride; it was built of logs, cemented inside, and had three rooms and quite a cellar; but she had frozen her feet, how she could not tell, for there was a carpet on the floor, and she had not been out; but then the winter had been *so cold!* it was now six weeks since her feet were first frozen, and she could not yet walk upon them. She came out here in company with Dr. P. and she thought the day was so fine she would come and consult him about her sore ankles.

A cheering little spirit she seemed to be; telling many pleasant bits of her experience in house-keeping. As good luck would have it, Dr. P. came into the room where we were. He seemed very glad to see her; questioned her about her feet, which had neither stockings nor shoes upon them, but were wrapped carefully and securely in an abundance of flannel. He seemed quite anxious at some of her replies, and said she must go home with him and pass the night, the better to secure a fair chance to examine the poor feet. The team was again brought to the door; the little lady lifted carefully into the seat, softened with a comforter; and, the last glimpse I ever expect to have of her, she was being faithfully escorted by her husband on one side, ox-whip in hand, and Dr. P. on the other, reining in his prancing, splendid, black horse, and pointing over the country to the place where his cabin stands. Through him I have since learned that she was from Cincinnati; the *only* daughter of a wealthy family, married without their knowledge or consent, while a school girl. Dear little "child-wife," who can ever avert the doom, sealed by your own thoughtless hand! There *are* men for whom, under some rare circumstances, so great a sacrifice might compensate, but this is not one of them. I see nothing before her but a life of protracted anxiety and suffering.

Disagreeable news begins to float up the river. A few persons from the East have arrived in town, and bring us word that a quantity of Sharpe's rifles and *four guns*, coming up the river, packed in carpenter-chests, and in charge of Boston men, were forcibly seized at Lexington and kept. The joke of it is, some little machinery belonging to each rifle was packed separately, was undiscovered by the pirates, and reached here in safety; so that if they fire the rifles, they will discharge at both ends! How many times, think you, will they fire them? One of the persons who had them in charge has gone to see Gov. Shannon, and demand an order for them. The Governor is now at Lecompton, a few miles farther up the river. What will that "gutta percha" man do in such a dilemma? If he refuses, then he acknowledges himself in favor of the robbers. If he grants the order, the robbers become his enemies. Poor "Gutta," I am always curious, and somewhat pitiful, too, when you have to decide a question.

Tell Ellen's "Uncle Ben" that I was very glad to receive the letter in which he bore a part. I hoped to answer it; but I have but little time to write, and very few conveniences for doing so — for a long while no table, nor chair, nor ink fit to mark paper with. Then, at first, I was very homesick. It seemed *chronic*, like a tooth-ache or a side-ache to which one has long been accustomed in a milder form; for I don't think I ever made even a temporary change of residence without suffering somewhat from it. In this instance I could do nothing to relieve it, and never told it to others; that is not my way. The heat through September was intense; the winds, even, seemed to come from a hot furnace. The sky was remarkable for its clear brightness. I felt almost as though I belonged to the owl family, it seemed so staring bright to me. Then, when the sun went down so grandly, so gracefully, behind the most exquisitely terraced hills in the far, far distance, and I would have refreshed myself by a cosey sit-down outside the cabin, to watch the stars and muse alone, there could nothing be found over this dreadfully cleared-up wilderness whereof a seat might be made! not a dear old pasture-knoll, or rock with its mossy cushion, or a wall holding so many nice flat stones, where one always is tempted to sit, alone, or with a friend, far into the night, or the stump of a tree, could this boasting, much-talked-of new world produce for my comfort, and remind me of home. The next great cause of discomfort to us was the lack of water. Accustomed to use it as freely as a duck — or, more to the point, perhaps, a goose — the doled-out pitcher-full at a hotel, with the thermometer at eighty or ninety, seemed wholly unendurable, though chargeable to the fault only of a certain condition of things, which time and more advanced " city improvements" could remedy.

For the cabin, water must be brought

nearly a quarter of a mile, unless taken from the river sleeping but a few rods off, and settled down to its narrowest bed by the dry hot summer, and cushioned round with shifting, strange-looking sand-bars, which partakes too much of the properties of the broader Missouri, into which it empties, for any Eastern house-keeper to risk her white cotton in it, or to use it willingly about her person.

I wonder if all this sounds like fault-finding? I mean it simply as a statement of facts, which I believe I started with to excuse myself for not writing to all my friends. How often they pass through my thoughts! or rather when they are absent from my thoughts it would be difficult to find out. Like the figures in a panorama, they come at my call, each making way for another, as in pictures turned by other machinery than the fancies of a busy brain. My promises to write come with them, like shadows on the wall; and then follows a discussion upon the weightiness of this or that reason for the neglect.

If I really had a conscience, I dare say these communings would be set down to its righteous upbraidings. But, mother, my present opinion is that I have no such attendant. Certainly, whatever labors I perform are a pleasure, usually; if not, they lie so close before me that intuition, I think, prompts to their accomplishment. Or, it may be, they intervene between me and something which I desire in my more interior nature to come at. Intuition helps: *this* puts spurs to my activity. What I do for my friends is a whole-hearted pleasure. Conscience does not help or hinder me, even to the taking off any amount of *me*, for their benefit. My friends! are they not the circumference of my heaven? Then surely it is no *duty-call* which makes me true, loving, and faithful to them. The world in general is an object of such intense sympathy and pity for all, that in its wrong-headedness it suffers, — as well as for all it loses, by resting on so low a moral and intellectual plane, — that naturally, not dutifully, I run all round, lifting a weary head here, or bathing an unsightly limb or visage there, till, weary with the energy I expend, I put myself upon the shelf for rest, saying very privately, whispering it close in the ears of this *me*, "What is *their* torture to *yours*? Has not your life been a long humiliation? a solitude, broken only upon its surface? a lone, helpless, womanly desolation, kept from dying out only by the often kindly grasp of the hand, the friendly recognition of the eye, or the more demonstrative letter, costing time, thought, and remembrance?

This childish, credulous *me*, thus flattered into a continued keeping upon the shelf, complacently makes out a case of justifiable repose for its future, keeping still a *negative* friendliness to the poor, pitiable portion of the world; but no more actual service. Where, I wonder, is my conscience now? If asleep, it is time a better sentinel was placed on guard over my soul!

Upon the whole, mother, my pen has struck out on the wrong road altogether. "Uncle Ben" did not wish a word on this highway: make it over to his brother; it will furnish him a theme for a sermon of rebuke to all conscienceless people.

This "Uncle Ben" of Ellen's, once before, wrote for my advice about the advantages to be gained by his going West; and I urged it with very many, to me then, strong reasons in favor of it. Our wise "sage of America" says: "Let a man speak what he thinks to-day, and to-morrow say what he believes; even if he contradicts the words of yesterday." Acting upon this permission, as well as the wider experience of to-day, I should take back whatever inducement at a former period, and in quite a state of ignorance, I might have then presented to him. At his age, (he will excuse me,) changes cannot be made in all one's habits of action and position, without pain; not to speak of loss, never to be regained—of ties, made strong with years, and strengthened by joy and sorrow. Few cultivated minds like his can safely go so far from everything they have known and joined sympathy with.

Did I ever tell you about a colony of emigrants, who went south from this place some seventy miles, or more or less? (I am never good with numbers.) Report says it was a most promising colony, and that they located in a most fertile, sunny region, where the rough winds do not have full play, as they do here. The summer was one of delightful weather—too fascinating for work, and too full of promise for sufficient preparation to be made against the coming winter-time. Autumn settled down with damp nights and heavy dews. The fever and ague spread among them all. The clergyman and his family were all down with it.

One day a brother clergyman, from New England—who had taken up the time of his summer vacation in coming to see his friend, and gratify his desire to see the country—found his way to the colony, and to the humble cabin of his friend. Rather a sad meeting it was; for there was no one able to provide for his comfort or their own. He cut wood for the fire—made his own coffee—and provided for his horse. While taking his own refreshment, there came in a poor, old, sick-looking man, who could hardly carry himself about, to borrow a shovel for the purpose of digging a grave for another man, who, he said, had just died; and on further inquiry, replied, that he was the only person left at all able to perform the service. The visitor "lifted up his voice and wept," repeating to himself, "I never could have believed in such a state of things without coming here to see it!" As soon as the clergyman and his family were well enough to be moved, they were brought to Lawrence.

The first time I saw them, a young lad, the only son of his mother, was suffering from a fit of the ague, wrapped up in blankets upon a lounge. The mother, a fair, gentle English woman, sat in an adjoining room, sewing together the breadths of a comforter. The only cabin they could obtain was a poor affair, leaking badly, and partly covered with cotton cloth. This little fellow worked with right good will to keep wood cut for the fire, as soon as he was able; but the weather came on so cold that fire made but little impression. At last, when the winter was far spent, a very comfortable house was made ready for them. The lady, however, had fastened upon her a serious cough, before the relief of warm air was granted to her. Hopes were entertained that spring would restore all she had lost through the winter. When, very suddenly, last week, the young lad was siezed with fever and total delirium. He survived but a few days. And in less than a week, his sorrow-stricken mother passed away also. All who now remain, are the father, a daughter about seventeen, and a pretty little pet, in the shape of a little girl about five years old. They came to stay with Typhoid, until preparations could be made for them to return east. The little girl still has turns of ague, but a change of climate will probably restore her.

This young boy's history reminds me of another lad, still younger, who has been an object of a great deal of interest to many persons among us. I cannot recall his name—for we all call him "Bub." When L. was travelling over the territory, at some place where he stopped he heard a conversation about this little boy, eleven years of age, who came out with his father to look about for a place of settlement. The father grew sick, and in order to provide for the boy, commenced a return journey. One night they put up, for the night only; but it proved the last of his life. The poor little orphan was completely crushed under the weight of a grief and desolation so dreadful. L. was so interested in the case, especially as they were Massachusetts people, that he made arrangements for the boy to be brought to Lawrence. As soon as he arrived here, I went in often to see him. He always met me with a smile, but made no conversation about the past. I'm sure I could not ask him any questions directly personal — sorrow seems so sacred. He is remarkably interesting in person; has more than the usual share of beauty; and, through his periods of almost daily fever or ague, he never frets nor exacts much from others. Indeed, the strange, bewildering loneliness of his position seems to have paralyzed every childish emotion. Sitting in a hard, ugly chair, close to the stove, when the chill is upon him, it is pleasant to witness how the roughest, sternest nature is softened when brought close to the same stove for warmth. "Well, Bub, are you better to-day?" comes in tones so truly sympathetic that the child-heart leaps up to answer.

Now there arrives from the East (that much-loved "land of Egypt" to every wandering Israelite in this far-off, strange land) a man whom we all love and honor — to whom we all look, as to a sheet-anchor in a storm. General Pomeroy gives both warmth and light to the parlor of the miniature "Cincinnati House." He loves children—*they* know by intuition who does; and this desolate little boy gives his unresisting hand into the great brown palm of the General, while, as the evening settles down into approaching night, and people pass out from the room usually so crowded, the kind-hearted man touches with so much tenderness the "aching cord" of his little companion, that the fountain of tears breaks open like a long pent-up flood. The little hand is covered with another brown palm—smoothed gently, and time given for all the relief which sobs and tears can bestow. Now follows, naturally, the story of his departure from home with his father—all the details of their long journey—the coming sickness—the final death of the father. Poor little fellow! It would have melted the stoutest heart to hear his unaffected, simple statement of the, to him, awful tragedy. Questions came often from the General, as well as words of comfort, in a voice gentle as that of a loving mother.

This man, with a heart in which the milk of human kindness had not been permitted to become acid, came down to the simple plane of the child's mind; took this great dilemma of his young life in hand, and solved it for him. He repeated his mother's name over and over again to him, until the poor little fellow became accustomed to the sound, and could repeat it himself without shrinking, and Hope lifted itself from the torpor of many a long day. Gen. Pomeroy promised to see him safe home to his mother; but not now. He must get well first; and for this purpose he would get him boarded at Dr. Barber's, long known as a missionary among the Indians, and well skilled in the treatment of diseases of the country. His mother should be written to immediately; and, when the warm spring weather came, he should be conducted to her.

All the while I am gathering to myself beautiful expositions of character like what I have just related. They are *riches* to me, in this far-off land, where there has been so much to disturb and irritate everybody. I turn from them with a sort of unutterable soul-sickness, to watch the dark clouds heaving up over our hopeful sky, from our heartless, poor-apology of a neighbor, Missouri. You will remember this, as the month when our *own* legislative body is to meet. We womenkind look with fear and trembling upon the departure of so many of our strong men to Topeka. If it was located between us and Missouri, I think we might enjoy the gathering together of this political machinery for the very laudable purpose of making laws for our protection. But Topeka is twenty-five miles farther up the river. I remember very well that in the winter, when Gen. L. hesitated about accepting an invitation to pass a portion of the cold winter with a friend in Missouri, "Sheriff Jones," judging, rightly enough, that it was as a soldier he hesitated, said, very decidedly: "I give you my word, as a man of honor, this people will be free from all invasion for the next six weeks."

Whatever faults the sheriff has, and however strong his prejudices may be against us unfortunate New Englanders, he pledged himself in a way not to be doubted; and he must have had good reason for limiting the time. That time is now up, and our people are assuming to take care of themselves. "Uncle Sam" feeds Missouri with sugar plums; but our cry, to be allowed to earn bread for ourselves, is not heard. What then can we do? Justice has fled entirely out of the country. The position of our people has reached the highest point of *heroic desolation.* Now we must " put our trust in God, and keep our *powder dry.*"

I hope you will read Gov. Robinson's message. It does not sound much like the voice of a reckless renegade. I feel very proud of it. Fifty years from now it will read quite as well, "I reckon," as anything Frank Pierce has had to offer on this subject. You will see, too, that "his excellency, Gutta Percha" is on his way back here; and, to arrest our wise men and take them all to pay a visit to Washington! I only hope he will have courage to do it. Many of them are worthy to fill high places at the seat of government, and only need to be seen that this may be acknowledged. Most solemnly, I declare to you, that I do not see any reason at all why this people have been so beset by an adjoining State. Everybody here seems disposed to mind their own business and let other folks alone. The quarrel in this instance is all on one side. We do not need couriers to bring us intelligence of Missouri's purposes concerning us. We feel it in the opposing sphere of the air around us. We hear it in the broken bits of talk, the awful oaths poured out upon the heads of all "Yankees"—which includes everybody east of the Mississippi and north of the Ohio. I smile at this wholesale contempt for us and the land of our birth; I smile, too, at the former narrowness of my views, when Boston seemed to me quite a place; its sons and daughters noble, aye, almost royal, by the right of persevering, successful effort. And, notwithstanding the new face with which my dear old home is here presented to me, I hug my prejudices the closer. I am not only proud, but thankful, very thankful, that New England is the land of my birth. Her laws and institutions are dearer to us than ever before; and Kansas, without a similar elevating basis of social and moral restraint, would not be worth travelling two thousand miles to secure.

Young as she is, Kansas is not without her "Moses and Aaron," to create and expound a code of laws suitable to meet her necessities, and worthy the epoch in which she appears before the public. Leave her in freedom to gather about her what she feels the need of, and even *you* will live to hear of her harmonious completeness and social comfort.

But if Kansas is to be the battle-field whereon all the exciting questions agitating the whole country are to be fought, in the name of all humanity, send " Wise men from the East" to do the work. We who came here to make *homes*, have already encountered quite a sufficiency of hardship to make our homes dear to us when they are made secure; quite enough of unkindness on the part of our neighbors, to settle, for a period at least, the question of " hospitality and chivalry."

I believe I have told you of the continual annoyance we experience from having boxes, packages, and goods generally, overhauled while coming up the river, or after they arrive at Kansas City. The last article looked upon as suspicious was a box containing a piano! I yesterday saw Professor Daniels, of Wisconsin. He informed me that while at St. Louis he saw several hundred men from the South, " armed and equipped" for Kansas! I think I shall go back to Massachusetts, for the present. I am heart-sick at all this fuss—and in the spring-time, too, when everything is beginning to look so hopeful and bright for the poor immigrants. Ploughs are out, making furrows in the smooth old prairies; while everywhere can be seen oxen and cows, with their noses close to the earth, pulling at the young blades of grass. There is a great stir, too, among the house-builders. Everybody is busy. I will not believe that better days are not in store for this sorely-tried and badly-used people. Frank Pierce can't live forever; and, after him, we must hope and pray for a "Joseph," who can hold the reins of government evenly, and unite contending parties by the strong bond of mutual safety.

Let me hear from you again very soon, and oblige your affectionate daughter,

H. A. R.

MISCELLANEOUS LETTERS.*

LAWRENCE, K. T. Nov., 1855.

HON. CHARLES SUMNER:

My Dear Sir, — Waiting to-night in my cabin, for L—— and C—— to come in for their supper, L—— surprised me, coming in alone to ask if he might bring home Judge S. to tea; which of course was only a pleasure to me, if it added at all to the comfort of any one engaged in the wearisome work of taking care of this "Yankee" settlement.

While sitting at the "board," L—— explained to me the necessity of sending some person immediately to Washington; and, would I write to *you,* or any other person I knew there? so that all the light possible to throw upon our present position might be

---

* The following letters are added by particular request, as throwing some rays of light upon Kansas Life, not so clearly detailed in the journal. I have also since learned that Mrs. Barbour has lost all consciousness, is dressed and fed as a child : her suffering is over ; her mind totally paralized.

given? I can hardly refuse; and yet I feel wholly unequal to, and quite out of place on a subject of so much importance.

Judging from my own impressions, I fear you Eastern people hardly do justice to the patient forbearance and long suffering of Kansas immigrants. Here in Lawrence, no week has ever passed without more or less insult and contumely thrown at our people by our nearest neighbors, the Missourians. We never ride, even within our own territory, and meet them, but our ears are pained with words too wicked to repeat. And they shoot at defenceless people with as much cool indifference as they would at partridges or prairie chickens.

My poor woman's-head does not pretend to sift, or unravel this state of things. I am only cognizant of the present sad and dangerous condition in which, as a town, we find ourselves. You who are wise and benevolent should be able to help us who are so defenceless, and so far removed from the ordinary means of helping ourselves. Perhaps, like many other "wise men," you may have imbibed the impression that Lawrence is a good-for-nothing fellow, always putting himself in the way disagreeably, or treading upon his neighbor's corns; if so, I wish I might be able to disabuse you of any such injustice. Lawrence is a hard-working, money-loving, mind-your-own-business sort of person; who, if it would not pay a good profit, probably would not take the time or trouble to look at or travel into his nearest neighbor's inhospitable domain. Through the most of this month, there has been more quiet and freedom from annoyance, than for many a week previous. Elections were over; the Free-State people had shown themselves three to one, and the question *seemed* to be at rest. But it was a mere *seeming*, a lull before a storm. There is not, there has not been, a single cabin *safe* from outrage *anywhere* in the territory for the two past weeks. Without the slightest provocation, men are cut down, leaving families in lone places without any protection; our cattle are taken; teams of freight stopped on the public way, and all the merchandize handled over, to see what it contains. Ammunition withdrawn, and then the luckless wagoner sent on his way. Market-men, too, coming to bring us apples, and potatoes, and flour, are forbidden to proceed. Gentlemen whom I know and honor, some of them simply visitors, riding in their own carriages up from Kansas City, find their horses' heads seized, while beastly, half-drunk Missourians demand their business, and a *pledge* that they will not tell Lawrence people how near armed men are camping around them.

It gives me pleasure to be able to affirm that I have known of no outrage exciting to this on the part of these poor, hard-struggling immigrants. I can but believe it to be wholly the result of bitter opposition to Eastern people, having the prospective chance of a fee-simple in the fair and beautiful hills and plains of Kansas. I see and believe that this feeling has been strong enough to lead Missouri to put forth her mean and treacherous hand, with the will to tear up by the roots every settlement where the southern mark is not stamped upon its inhabitants. O, men of Congress! where is the use of your assembling together, if not for the good of those who are in need of your aid?

Last night a strong and noble specimen of

a man passed close by our cabin on his watch. I heard his cheerful voice, and the slow tramp of his horse, as though he did not wish to disturb our sleep, but only to assure us of safety. To-day, while off of duty, he is cut down as a butcher would an ox. Long before this reaches you, other victims will sleep their last sleep. Our houses are no protection. There is hardly a cabin which a strong man could not tear down.

Let me add, as a relief to myself, that I am proud of Kansas and Kansas men and women. They live in cabins; wear shabby clothes, and rusty boots; their whole appearance offends my intuitive love for whatsoever is beautiful, orderly, and graceful; but the energy, courage, good judgment, and noble magnanimity shown in these nights and days of danger, sweep away all antecedents. I see them in the majesty and power of a true and noble manhood.

H. A. R.

LAWRENCE, K. T., 8TH DEC., 1855.

MY DEAR MR. M.,— You are very kind to write to me twice without hearing from me between-whiles. I think I must have given quite a hapless picture of our condition to excite so much commiseration. But I made up my mind, when I left home, to give the "outs" of Kansas life, for I felt quite sure we had never heard them.

I am glad to be again able to write to you, and that my "old cheerful way" has come back with the putting on of my usual strength; and also, that I still have a fund of cheerful words for those who need them so much.

A— has been the sickest patient, with one exception, I have seen. There seemed, for a week, almost no chance of her recovery; and she is now a long, skinny animal, in whom you would find hard work to recognize the round-faced, romping little girl who was so long your pupil; but there is now everything to give us hope that she will recover.

E— is suffering from the badly-cooked food and awful accommodations of last winter;

added to which he has been for months a nurse and watchman for the sick, and finds himself listless and easily tired out.

The cabin is papered with many thicknesses of newspapers; glass has taken the place of cloth, for windows; and the cotton door has given place to one made of walnut. It is a funny looking place; and I wish, as a matter of mere curiosity, aside from the desire to see you, you could all look in and call as of old.

So much for us, personally; which I am sure it has been difficult for me to come back to or hunt up, amid all we have to do and plan for.

Long before this reaches you, the note of alarm will have sounded among you, and you will tremble for our safety. We are now a city under martial law. Many men are on guard every night; and the unfinished hotel is the head-quarters of our Commander-in-Chief, Dr. Robinson, where he and his aids, with an armed force, sleep, and have done so for more than a week. Our friend General Pomeroy is a prisoner of war in the camp, six miles east of us. As soon as this was known, martial law was instituted. Now it will be known who comes and goes. So far, everything has been done to defend the town; but not to provoke blood-shed. General Robinson grows with our needs; and there is as fine a set of men now assembled as council of war, in the rude hotel, as could probably be gathered in any state in the Union. Young men of education, who, had they remained in old towns and cities, would have passed through life as agreeable, refined, literary men, of midling rank in some profession — transplanted here — stripped of all the appointments of effeminacy — pushed to exertion, with the penalty of starvation affixed — driven, by Missourians, to stand up tall, or be run down — to fire, or be shot — how can they help putting forth new powers? There is still another class here — men of the wisdom which comes even to the stupid, with age — whom the turning of the wheel of fortune has left *poor*. They renew life in this new state of things. Ministers of the gospel, even, are in the ranks to-day, at the drill. Gray hairs float in the breeze over furrowed brows, mounted on horses that show they have come a long journey from farther up the country. L. brought home one with him, to partake of our cabin fare, who came here from New Jersey, and now lives at Leavenworth. Perhaps I may as well add, for the amusement of your girls, that they took refreshment from a walnut board, made into a cross-legged table, pushed, for want of room, half way under the shelf where I keep my dishes. The tea was from Mr. Kendall's store at home, which the gentleman pronounced the best he had tasted in the territory, and gave me the better proof by handing his cup many times to be filled: In the midst of all this, I ask L. if there is danger of famine. He replies, with his merry laugh, "One hundred bushels of corn were ground last night." One man, who fastens his horse at our stand, told me he should have four thousand bushels of corn from his claim. So you can see that we can stand something of a seige.

To-day, Gov. Shannon and Gen. Robinson are trying to make peace on some satisfactory terms to all parties. I am no politician, do not understand the ground of our offence, and cannot give you properly the results.

Tell D. the "shake-down" provided for him has rarely been vacant at all. H. A. R.

LAWRENCE, K. T., 5TH FEB., 1856.

MY DEAR MRS. M.,—I always like to think there is a time for all things which we ought to do, or that it is our lawful pleasure to do; so, very many times in the autumn, after your very kind note, I said to myself, "the day or hour to give to Mrs. M. must be hereabouts." But the close-crowding of things to be done for some one, made it quite impossible for me to give aught to you and very many other friends, except long periods of thought, while watching in silence over the sick, or going through the routine of cabin house-keeping.

Our cabin is fifteen feet square, with a nice room over it. Our common clothing hangs over the walls, around the corners appropriated to our beds. Opposite these opens the door, at the right side of which are shelves of black walnut, very roughly put up, for dishes, and a table of the same beautiful wood. On the left side are arranged the materials for cooking; while pendant from the beams overhead, hang, in curious proximity, venison, beef, the potato-basket, bags for beans, nice dried-apple, and patches, together with workbaskets.

The earth, everywhere where the turf is off, is the blackest and richest of garden-loam. When moistened by rain or heavy dew, it becomes like ink and flower. This, applied with many feet to the cotton boards, creates a decidedly brown color, which no person, after a week's experience, would ever attempt to remove with any other implement than a broom.

For a new country, this is surprisingly well provided with a variety of food. We get very fine, large apples in the fall, for a dollar a bushel; sweet potatoes, for a quarter more. These things are brought fifty miles, over deep ravines which would quite frighten you to look into.

The west portion of Missouri is mostly inhabited with a partially civilized race, fifty years behind you in all manner of improvements. In November a wagon load of thirty bushels of apples, none of which would measure less than a pint bowl, and one of which could hardly be stowed in a pie, were sold in this market at the price just mentioned.

They were a red-striped apple, somewhat like the "Baldwin" in appearance. The taste of all this fruit is peculiar; and though they vary in color, size and value, this flavor in a degree pervades them all. Another noticeable fact is their total freedom from worms. Much of this fruit is raised by the Indians of this Territory. The hard-working immigrants have, even during this first summer of their new life, raised an abundance of potatoes, squashes, pumpkins, tomatoes, together with a large amount of corn. We bought for our cow, pumpkins for nine shillings a hundred. Some of these things grow to an immense size. Squashes weighing from a hundred to a hundred and fifty pounds. A— says, one she saw at the hotel was large enough for a cradle. Corn-meal has sold at the same price of apples. It is very much nicer than any I ever saw before — sweet, delicate, as white as rice. A hot corn-cake never leaves a crumb to tell of its existence. The meats of the country are cheap, compared with Eastern prices. Flour is high, and never of the best quality. Butter poor, and thirty cents a pound. Milk, ten cents a quart, two thirds of the year.

Every advantage is taken of the necessities of new comers.

You will perceive that I have taken you back to the months of Autumn, the date and subject of your letter. Half the time, too, (and I am sure you will excuse it) it has seeemed as I write, as though I was talking to your father, whose love for moral and political economy, in connection with every portion of his country, seems to reach and animate me.

You will hear, by other ways, of the necessary guard about our ill-fated little town. All that serves us now is the severity of cold winter weather and the deep snow, still dropping steadily; as though, in the absence of all pity in Congress, and all help from good men in the States, it would cover us securely with its shroud-like mantle.

How kind it is of you, to remember so constantly one whose life is almost too broken to come in the range of what you see and hear. H. A. R.

ELM HALL, BROOKLINE, May 29, 1856.

To J. M. W. ESQ.,
Independence, Mo.

My Dear Sir, — I have not forgotten the promise I made, to send you a paper from Boston, as a token of our safe arrival home. I suppose an apology will seem to you very much in want of another to cover it, when I say, — all the papers I read contained some items of intelligence about your State which it did not seem courteous for me to place upon your table.

Could I have given them to you personally, I dare say we should have talked the contents over as kindly and rationally as we did the same subject during those long, quiet, sunny days when together we "steamed" down your beautifully wide and grand old river.

Our party of returning emigrants had just come out from under the weight of evil foreboding, which rested alike upon everybody in Kansas. We gave ourselves up to the beauty of river-journeying and the pleasant society of your excursion-party of Missourians.

Almost always, in looking back, we discover more to mourn over than to rejoice in. Our self-gratulation is at the escapes we make from wrong, rather than the positive good we do. But this journey along the turbid waters of the Missouri, and subsequently in the cars to Indianapolis, the kindness we received, the good feeling expressed by you and most certainly felt by us, keep that week of adventure pleasantly green and fresh in my memory.

It was a phase of Missouri character quite unlike the brutal specimens we had seen and lived in constant fear of for a long winter, and compelled me almost into the belief that I had awakened from the horrors of the nightmare. And had there been no new outrage to remind us of what we had suffered from our cruel neighbors, that source of suffering would in time have been wholly forgotten, or remembered only as the result of misapprehension on the part of your people.

I am sorry now that I did not write to you immediately after my return home. I should have had so many pleasant things to say. My faith in the race was quickened into new life by our friendly conversations. I now remember them sadly, as numbered with many other states of the strongest trust in man,—passed away to return no more.

Now, I wish to remind you of graphic descriptions given by different members of our party, of Kansas. Let me take you by the hand and go with you to the thrifty little town of Lawrence. Dear little village of cabins! a petted "Benjamin" to those of us who are no longer young. Stand outside my cabin, and look with me and listen. The sun sinks down with a train of glory never surpassed in any country. Many cabins nestle close to the ground before you, and hundreds of people trace their way to their own, busy with their own thoughts, plans and purposes for the future.

The laborer places away his hod, his trowel and his hammer. He sings as he plods along, for his work is done and his supper is ready. How still the place is, broken now only by the distant tinkle of the cow-bell. Night unfolds her tent-like curtain of darkness. Listen! "while he, the man of prayer, commends to God the weary here;" across the stillness floats his voice, subdued with reverence, and earnest with thanksgiving and supplication. He asks that "those who wait to shed innocent blood may be forgiven, and that the hearts of unfeeling strangers may be turned towards us." He gives thanks for returning Spring. We return to our poor cabins full of peace.

—The last month of spring is come. Hope springs anew in hearts almost broken. The hotel is finished. Strangers now have a home in good earnest, for there never was a more hospitable landlord than Mr. Eldridge. Take heart, little city of immigrants, "for the time for the singing of birds is come," and you are not destroyed.—The last week of spring is here, and where, alas! is the little defenceless town?

What a boiling, surging chaldron your Missouri must be, to pour over a scum of robbers and assassins so often into a neighboring territory! Surely, after such a clarifying, there ought to remain an element clear, strong, and powerful, to work righteousness, justice, and mercy. If there is any such element, it seems to be hid and useless; else it would come to our rescue.

Stretching along the north side of Lawrence, sweeps the Kansas River, making an impassible barrier between us and our friends, the Deleware Indians. Our southern limit is walled in by Mount Oread; upon the top of which stretches a dark line of Missourians. On the same highland is the house of Gov. Robinson; and midway from its base stands the unfinished church. East and west you will see a still more fearful army of armed men. Sweeping across the prairies, too, are groups of horsemen. Fastened in the town are tents of United States troops. All this parade is against us! incredible as it seems. What we have done, to be thus proscribed by Missouri, and, worse than all, unheeded by our President, it will certainly take the crooked head of a statesman to unravel. I willingly leave it to you lawyers. We, who suffer from this protracted apprehension, know very well what the sensation is. History will take account of the facts, in this unparalleled confusion of *right* and *wrong*. History will immortalize the brave and true men who had the courage to give up their arms and surrender, when successful resistance to outrage was no longer possible. But only the "Recording Angel" keeps a truthful reckoning of the pitiful cry from the hopeless, despairing women, and frightened, bewildered children.

Sheriffs Jones and Donaldson ate of our bread and drank of our cup, and then, Judas-like, straightway went forth to destroy us.

The brave boy, who stood by us and gave them welcome, now sees, for the second time, his cabin destroyed by your people. God only knows if his life is spared. His last words to me were: "Mother, go back to Boston; I never knew how to value the laws of old Massachusetts till I came out here. Never you fear for me, mother; I must stand in my lot. Shouldn't you be ashamed of me if I went away?" And the answer was, "YES, MY SON."

Now I perceive more fully the rare wisdom of this boy-man.

On the 22d of May, your mob closed in around our little town. Spider-like, they wove their web of destruction.

For two weeks, the most intense anxiety

and fear have worn out the strength and hearts of our people. After midnight, when, if ever, the weary watcher falls asleep, there is a startling, wolf-like whoop, penetrating every soul of man, woman or child, and they spring to their feet. Day has not yet dawned; but through the dim light preceding morning, may be seen the approaching army of madmen. Some little show of order is preserved, while a few more sham arrests are made — thus to secure all the leading men of the town. This done, all houses are broken into; everything of value stolen; all left behind, unsuitable to move, broken up. The next step was to assemble in Massachusetts Street, front of the hotel, with cannon. On the opposite side of the street stood a cabin, occupied by Mr. Brown, editor of the "Herald of Freedom;" and in the rear of the cabin, a fine stone building, three stories high, built, under great difficulty, and just finished, for a printing office. Close at the side of the hotel stood another cabin, occupied by Mrs. Wood, a beautiful young woman, wife of D. N. Wood, who is a prisoner. A printing office joined this cabin. In the centre of these proscribed buildings were placed the cannon, and charge followed charge upon the strong stone hotel. The sturdy walls looked cooly at the fuss and noise, but did not move nor tremble. Now platoons fired at the windows of it. The sheriff refused any time, or aid, to remove women or children. This hotel had been built as a pleasant home for strangers; and also as a place of safety to all of us in the time of danger. But now, in the utmost terror, these people flee from it, and from the sheriff and his posse. Along the banks of the river they run wildly, creeping into deep ravines to hide from the fury of the drunken men.

Dear little children—God help them! What compensation can life ever give to atone for this page of awful reality?

My dear sir, you have but to imagine your *own wife* and *beautiful boy* among these exiles, to give force to the picture, and stir aright your sympathy. This wrong cries aloud— by blood, rapine, and robbery—to just Heaven for redress. In my humble opinion there is no page of history so revolting as this; and the wounds are doubly bitter because they come from a SISTER STATE.

After placing powder in the cellar, the hotel surrendered. The printing presses were laid to rest in the river; and at last the post office gave up its honored credentials of office to those hired assassins of that most *unmitigated calamity* Heaven ever suffered upon the earth — FRANKLIN PIERCE.

We who have escaped alive are in painful uncertainty of the small notes in this sad history. Some of us have risked our all in that territory, and LOST ALL. Our sons, if living, may now be hungry and naked; yet we have no power to reach and succor them.

The walls of this pleasant chamber have seemed like a prison, as, in the hours when others sleep, I walk up and down it; while every thought and affection overleaps your truly dreadful State, to stoop, in tearful sympathy, over the forsaken, dying Lawrence.

I open the blinds, and look forth for the early morning, "when the day begins to dawn;" but my thoughts will not come home. I now remember, and enter into the states of those women of old, who stood at the cross and the sepulchre weeping, and to whom was given the voice of hope and consolation, in these words: "He is not here, but risen!"

Thought goes back a page farther in the old history, when two women wept over the grave of their only brother, and Jesus, standing by, "wept" also. He did not give us the example of expending all his sympathy in tears; no! "With a loud voice he said, 'Lazarus, come forth!'"

Lawrence is dead! but as surely as there is justice in Heaven, this death by violence, wholly unprovoked, will be avenged. As surely as there are disciples of Jesus still doing his work on the earth, so surely shall this martyrdom become the seed of a true church, to lighten the heathen world about it.

Lawrence shall hear the words, spoken by the up-rising better nature of man, saying, "come forth!" and the glory of the newly-built city shall far surpass the degredation of its present ruin.

I do not ask you to excuse the sorry words dropping from my pen. I hold you still by the hand, and, as your superior in years, demand your rational attention. You are young, earnest, and honest. I believe you truly desire to do what is right.

Lawrence is dead! toll the bells all over your State, for the skirts of your garments are dripping with blood. This is *murder*, deliberately planned, and coolly carried out. Which of you did it? You are a citizen of Missouri. Call your people together, and charge the deed where it belongs. There is restitution to be made.

As a State, pray try the experiment for once, of high minded magnanimity. If there is anywhere within your precints a record of Jewish Laws, originally written upon "two tables of stone," and, by common consent, called "The Ten Commandments" — if the words of Jesus, "a new commandment give I unto you, that ye love one another," are to to be found within your territory — take them before your "wise men," for action. Your people have outraged society by the crimes of murder, arson, and robbery. No power of yours can give us back the slain! Our great Master gives us the prayer to meet your case, and we will use it always when we remember you: "Father, forgive them, for they know not what they do."

The houses you have burnt you can rebuild;

and the goods you have stolen, you can restore. You as a State, are rich and strong; we were poor and weak, and from us you have taken the little that we had. We went to Kansas to make homes; and violated no law by so doing. We do not intend to give up the plan of remaining; and when you are better acquainted with us proscribed Yankees, your animosity will have passed away. Hoping that you will be able and willing to redeem your name from dishonor among the States, I remain yours very truly,

H. A. R.